CATCH-67

CATCH-67

THE LEFT, THE RIGHT, AND THE LEGACY OF THE SIX-DAY WAR

MICAH GOODMAN

TRANSLATED BY EYLON LEVY

Yale UNIVERSITY PRESS

NEW HAVEN & LONDON

Published with assistance from the Louis Stern Memorial Fund.

Yale University Press books may be purchased in quantity for educational, business, or promotional use. For information, please e-mail sales.press@yale.edu (U.S. office) or sales@yaleup.co.uk (U.K. office).

Set in Meridien and Futura types by Integrated Publishing Solutions, Grand Rapids, Michigan.
Printed in the United States of America.

Library of Congress Control Number: 2018938413
ISBN 978-0-300-23674-3 (hardcover : alk. paper)

A catalogue record for this book is available from the British Library.

This paper meets the requirements of ANSI/NISO Z39.48–1992 (Permanence of Paper).

10 9 8 7 6 5 4 3 2 1

This book is dedicated to my dear friend, the late Sari Rubinstein.

CONTENTS

PREFACE TO THE ENGLISH EDITION

The Arab-Israeli conflict plays such a dominant role in the Israeli consciousness that it has all but taken over. While Israelis do care about questions of taxation, socioeconomic inequality, and the relationship between religion and state, these issues rarely determine how they vote. Israelis vote for the parties that represent their positions on the conflict. The monopoly of the conflict within political discourse in Israel remains one of the unacknowledged consequences of the Six-Day War.

How can the conflict be solved? Where should Israel's eastern border run? What will be the fate of Jerusalem? And what of the settlements? Proponents on both Israel's left and right have been arguing about these questions, and many others, for the past fifty years; various attempts have been made to end the conflict, each reaching a dead end. The conflict remains active, and the debate over what to do about it continues to hurt Israeli society from within.

Catch-67 is not about the Arab-Israeli conflict as such, but rather about the debate inside Israel about it. My journey into Israel's national political debate will be a journey into the heart of Israeli society. This debate is stormy, even fiery—but no one can hope to understand Israel without understanding the main argument that is being had within Israeli society.

The problem with the current state of political debate is not confined to Israel or the Arab-Israeli conflict. Across much of Europe and the United States, political debate has stopped functioning. What is meant by a "functional" political debate? A disagreement between people each of whom believes the other is wrong: I think you are wrong, and you think I am wrong. That's how a good political debate ought to work. But what if I think you are not only wrong but evil? Reasonable disagreement collapses. Social media tend to amplify this dynamic. People are increasingly concerned with *labeling* others, instead of thinking about their arguments. When they are exposed to new political ideas, they seldom think about whether the ideas are right or wrong—instead they ask, for example, whether they are liberal or conservative. Such people categorize ideas as a means of determining how to think about them. The effort to understand political arguments has been replaced by the desire to assign them to narrow categories.

Such are the voices heard on social media in Israel. Oftentimes, right-wingers think not only that left-wingers are wrong but that their openness to a territorial withdrawal makes them a threat to Israel, and perhaps even traitors. Oftentimes, left-wingers think not only that right-wingers are wrong but that their opposition to a two-state solution makes them a danger to Israeli society, and perhaps even fascists. The poisonous debate in Israel exemplifies the poisoning of political conversation around the world. When each side thinks that the other's beliefs are not only wrong but illegitimate, the capacity to listen vanishes, and reasonable disagreement collapses.

Consider the difference between Israelis' conversations about politics and their conversations about technology. Differences of opinion about technological matters are aired with an openness that has created an elastic, energetic, and effective dialogue. As a result, Israelis have generated a tremendous amount of technological innovation in the past two decades, and Israel is known worldwide as an incubator for new ideas and out-of-the-box thinking. Readers of this book might be surprised to learn that such a small country has produced more startup companies per capita than any major European nation.

In recent years, millions of people from around the world have visited Israel to learn about creativity and entrepreneurship from the Startup Nation. Visitors used to come to Israel primarily for its holy sites, such as the Western Wall and Church of the Holy Sepulcher, but today many arrive to tour its companies, such as Waze and MobilEye. This is a new brand of tourism, and it tells a new story about the State of Israel. If people used to visit Israel for a look at the past, now they visit Israel for a glimpse of the future.

But among those international visitors eager to learn about technological innovation none come to learn about political innovation. With regard to the most pressing issue for the Israeli public, the conflict with the Palestinians, Israel's creative edge disappears. When it comes to solving the conflict, Israelis find themselves recycling the same ideas over and over again.

Much has been written about the secret of Israelis' creativity. That secret lies in a certain rare quality of conversation in Israel. Enter an Israeli company, and you will be confronted with open discussion, group brainstorming, and a fruitful exchange of ideas. New ideas are met with enthusiasm; new thoughts are welcomed with encouragement. This is how Israelis create a climate conducive to the flourishing of new ideas.

But in contrast to the technological conversation, the political conversation in Israel leads not to the exchange of ideas but to the exchange of blows. Israelis do not listen to each other—they blame each other. Such intolerance cannot create an environment for the generation of innovative thinking; it can only *block* innovative thinking. Israelis, who argue so creatively about technology, argue unproductively about politics. When conversation dries up, creativity dries up along with it.

I wrote this book originally in Hebrew for an Israeli readership. My purpose was to reflect back to Israelis their own arguments in a bid to heal their own national conversation. I wanted to show Israelis that for Israel to be politically and not just technologically groundbreaking, they needed not to try to *win* the political argument but first and foremost to try to *repair* the political argument.

Has this book achieved its goal in Israel? For now, it would appear not. *Catch-67* was one of the most widely read books in Israel in 2017. It was publicly discussed by the heads of all the major parties, as well as Israel's leading opinion makers. Nevertheless, the book has failed to change or even calm the political debate in Israel. Instead of healing discord, the book itself sparked discord. Many right-wing readers argued that I took a left-wing stance, while many left-wing readers argued that I favored a right-wing position. A book whose author begged its readers to rise above attempts to *categorize* was itself subjected to countless attempts at categorization.

Catch-67 focuses on the internal Israeli debate. As such, it contains analyses of different points of view and the deeper philosophies that underpin them. It is not a book about the Israeli-Palestinian conflict, and I provide little analysis of the internal debate among Palestinians. Nor is it a work of *hasbara*, an attempt to "defend" Israel, offering answers to various accusations hurled at Israel. I present neither a systematic treatment of the assaults on Israel's right to exist nor a defense of that right. This is a book about how Israelis think, and the overwhelming majority of Israelis are arguing not about Israel's right to exist but about its borders and its future. I did not write this book to defend Israel but to explain it.

In *Catch-67* I explore the philosophical foundations of the governing ideologies of the Israeli left and right, as well as the clash between them. Most important, however, I also look at a surprising consequence of this clash. Though few commentators address it, and many may not realize it, most Israelis today have lost their sense of political conviction. They no longer identify with the ideologies of the left or the right. Most Israelis have lost their sense of certainty and been plunged into confusion, an outcome that may come as a surprise to foreign observers of Israel. This book is an exploration of Israel's old ideologies and how they led to this newfound confusion. If we can understand how this confusion arose and what it is doing to Israeli society, I argue, we might see that it also presents an opportunity to move forward. Healing the fractured conversation about the conflict can pave a path toward new ideas that can help heal the conflict itself.

Micah Goodman
February 2018, Jerusalem

N

LEBANON

SYRIA

MEDITERRANEAN
SEA

• Haifa

Nazareth •

1949 Israel-Jordan
armistice line

• Nablus

WEST BANK

Jordan R.

Tel Aviv •
Jaffa •

• Ramallah

Jerusalem •

• Hebron

GAZA STRIP

• Beer Sheva

1949 Israel-Egypt
armistice line

ISRAEL

JORDAN

EGYPT

0	10	20	30	40	50 mi
0	20	40	60	80 km

Israel before 1967

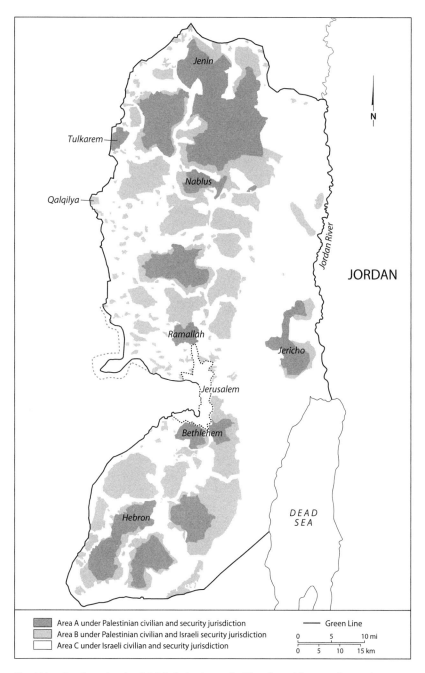

The West Bank under the 1995 Oslo Accords. The dotted lines indicate the boundary before 1967 (*left*) and Israeli-annexed East Jerusalem (*right*).

CATCH-67

INTRODUCTION

Can the Israeli National Conversation Be Healed?

On the eve of the Six-Day War, Israel formed a national unity government (a broad coalition of all major parties) for the first time in its history. Faced with an acute military threat from the United Arab Republic (a union of Egypt and Syria), not only was Israel's government united: the whole of Israeli society united as well, and a sense of solidarity spread among Jews across the country and throughout the world. This unity formed the backdrop for the greatest victory in Israel's history. In only six days of war, 5–10 June 1967, the Israel Defense Forces (IDF) defeated a coalition of Arab armies (after the Egyptian president Gamal Abdel Nasser persuaded Jordan, Iraq, and Syria to ally with him) and tripled the size of the country, capturing the Sinai Peninsula, the Golan Heights, the Gaza Strip, and the West Bank.

Yet the conquest of these territories ignited a painful debate within Israel itself: Should these new territories be settled by Jews, or should they rather be relinquished to the Arabs in exchange for peace? Those who dreamt of keeping the Land of Israel united clashed with those who dreamt of keeping it at peace, and the opponents tore Israeli society into two competing camps. The powerful sense of unity that had dominated on the eve of the war collapsed, ultimately, because of the results of that same war.

Much has changed since then in the relationship between Israel and the Palestinian Arabs who live in the territories conquered in 1967. Israel has suffered the outbreak of two intifadas, among other crises, as well as three major rounds of violence in the Gaza Strip. It has endured the fateful years that followed the Oslo Accords: the years of disengagement from Gaza and of repeated attempts to broker a permanent peace between the two sides. Not a single round of war secured victory, and not a single round of talks secured peace. But while these fruitless efforts to win victory or peace continued, an equally endless argument raged within Israel itself over where to draw the country's borders.

The territories conquered in just six days of conflict sparked a debate that has endured for fifty years.

Jewish tradition treats the fiftieth year as a jubilee: every fifty years, slaves are liberated from their masters, all debts forgiven, and all lands returned to their former owners. The jubilee is the moment when the clocks are reset. Socioeconomic inequalities created over the preceding fifty years are eliminated, and all distinctions of status between master and slave are wiped away. After fifty years, it is as if the world is created anew.

The jubilee year of the Six-Day War is an opportunity for Israelis to reset their internal argument and create their discourse anew. The opinions expressed and the arguments aired over the past fifty years have led both Israeli and Palestinian societies to a dead end. In biblical times, the fiftieth year was an opportunity for Jewish renewal, a chance for Jews to reexamine the basic assumptions of their political thought. But as a psychological precondition for reconfiguring their ways of thinking, Israelis must first adopt a radical change in the way they relate emotionally to those ways of thinking.

OUR EMOTIONAL RELATIONSHIP TO OUR OPINIONS

The temptations of consumerism offer an endless distraction in the modern world and can shape people's core identity. Citizens in a consumer society tend to develop emotional and even intimate relationships with their possessions. In the most extreme cases of materialism, people regard their possessions as parts of their beings, not merely things that they own.

Extreme materialism is similar to extreme idealism. Idealists struggle to differentiate themselves from their ideas. Their worldviews not only consist of collections of ideas but form an integral part of their identity. Idealists identify with their ideas just as materialists identify with their possessions. People who assimilate their opinions into their identity become closed to criticism of those opinions. As they see it, any objection to their views is an assault on their being.

Israel today is flooded with competing ideas. Israelis express a wide range of opinions on such matters as the economy and society or the role of religion in the state, and the clashes between their ideas provoke lively and even stormy debate. Nevertheless, Israelis have absorbed their viewpoints into their very identity on one topic alone—the Arab-Israeli conflict.

For Israelis, their opinions on the environment, say, or interest rates play a part in how they think. In contrast, their opinions on where to place Israel's eastern border form a part of *who they are.* An Israeli who believes in withdrawing to the lines of 4 June 1967 is a leftist. An Israeli who believes in settling the disputed territories is on the right. In contrast to other political opinions, these positions shape how Israelis define not only the world but themselves.

To object to an Israeli's position on the conflict is to object to his or her core identity. Therein lies the paradox: on the issue that matters to them the most, Israelis are the least capable of listening to one another.

The Israeli right believes that the ideas of the left are not just wrong but dangerous: a withdrawal from the mountains of Judea and Samaria would leave Israel shrunken, weakened, vulnerable, and doomed to physical destruction. The Israeli left believes that the ideas of the right are not just wrong but dangerous: a continued military and civilian presence in the disputed territories would leave Israel morally dilapidated, internationally isolated, and doomed to demographic destruction.

The right sees the left exactly as the left sees the right. The right is convinced that the left's vision will cause Israel's total collapse, and the left is convinced that the right's vision will cause Israel's total collapse. How can an Israeli on either the right or the left listen to a fellow citizen whose vision spells disaster for the entire country?

In Israel, the conversation about borders is unique among political arguments because of these two features: an Israeli's own opinions are a part of his or her identity, and others' opinions are a threat to his or her existence. The combination of these two characteristics has prevented either side from listening to the other and has caused the collapse of Israeli political dialogue.

Israelis do not view discussions of the conflict as a brain-storming exercise to provoke original thinking, challenge pre-conceptions, or nurture new and creative ideas. Israeli political debate becomes less an exchange of ideas than an affirmation of identities. The fiery tone of the debate has led to ideological and intellectual rigidity—a clearly disturbing result. The Arab-Israeli conflict is a complex subject, but the way Israelis think about it is not complex at all. What remains is an asymmetry between the profundity of the problem and the superficiality of the thinking it provokes.

The fiftieth year of this enduring conversation offers Israelis the opportunity to start over—but only if they have the courage to detach their opinions from their identities.

JEWISH DIALOGUE VERSUS ISRAELI DIALOGUE

One way to detach opinions from identities might be through inspiration from the Talmud, which describes a dispute between two leading schools of thought in the first century CE: Beit Sham-mai, the House of the scholar Shammai, and Beit Hillel, that of Rabbi Hillel. "For three years Beit Shammai and Beit Hillel dis-agreed," records the Talmud. "These said: The *halakha* [religious law] is in accordance with our opinion, and these said: The *halakha* is in accordance with our opinion. Ultimately, a Divine Voice emerged and proclaimed: Both these and those are the words of the living God. However, the *halakha* is in accordance with the opinion of Beit Hillel."[1] Who is correct: Beit Shammai or Beit Hillel? According to the Divine Voice, they are equally cor-rect. The opinions of both of them are "the words of the living God." But even though they are both right, they cannot both determine religious law, which follows Beit Hillel. How could this be? The Talmud explains:

> Since both these and those are the words of the living God, why were Beit Hillel privileged to have the *halakha* established in accordance with their opinion? The reason is that they were agreeable and forbearing, showing restraint when affronted, and when they taught the *halakha* they would teach both their own statements and the statements of Beit Shammai. Moreover, when they formulated their teachings and cited a dispute, they prioritized the statements of Beit Shammai to their own statements, in deference to Beit Shammai.[2]

Scholars belonging to Beit Shammai refused to hear or listen to the positions of Beit Hillel. They would study and teach their own positions exclusively. Scholars belonging to Beit Hillel, however, taught their own positions only after first hearing and listening to those of the rival Beit Shammai. In the end, God chose Beit Hillel to determine religious law because its scholars chose not to listen only to themselves. Ultimately, religious law is determined not by the side that is right but by the side that is willing to listen.

Listening, however, comes at a price. Beit Shammai did not change its positions even once during its many arguments with Beit Hillel—but Beit Hillel ended up backtracking and changing its positions several times, accepting the arguments of its rivals.[3] Listening means risking one's own beliefs. The scholars of Beit Hillel took the risk and therefore got to make the decision—not because they were always right but precisely because they were aware that they were not always right.

The school of Beit Hillel was neither full of doubt nor void of conviction. On the contrary, its scholars were firm in their beliefs and declared unambiguously, "The *halakha* is in accordance with our opinion." And still, despite the strength of their convictions, they refused to become intimately connected to those convictions. They were careful to keep a healthy distance between themselves and their opinions. This is the critical distance that prevents our opinions from completely taking over our identity.

This appealing Talmudic anecdote teaches that religious law is determined, paradoxically, by those who are not wedded to their own beliefs. Could this Talmudic paradox serve as a model for modern Israel? Could the healthy self-doubt of Beit Hillel pierce the armor of modern Israeli political discourse? For Israelis to rehabilitate their national conversation about the conflict, they must first repair their own emotional relationship to their own opinions. The emotional tempest undermining discussion of the conflict, however, pales in comparison with the emotional tempest of the conflict itself.

THE EMOTIONAL TRAP

The rift between Israelis and Palestinians is perpetuated by a destructive psychological dynamic. The clash between these two nations is also a clash of emotions. The dominant emotion among Israelis is fear. Israelis fear the Palestinians.[4] This fear is ancient, deep, and common to Israelis of all political stripes. The sound of someone speaking Arabic sets off alarm bells for left-wing and right-wing Israelis alike. The dominant emotion among Palestinians is not fear but humiliation.[5] Palestinians are not afraid of Israelis, but they feel humiliated by them. The conflict between these two nations is a clash of emotions—specifically, a painful confrontation between fear and humiliation.

These emotions nurture and aggravate one another. The Israelis' fear of Palestinians pushes them to take defensive steps, such as placing restrictions on Palestinians' movement, delaying their passage through checkpoints, and questioning them at the entrances to public places. The Palestinians' sense of humiliation grows deeper as a result of these actions. But the destructive dynamic does not end here. This humiliation enflames the existing feelings of hatred and anger, and creates a climate that breeds violence—violence that in turn heightens the Israelis' sense of fear. Tragically, the Israelis' sense of fear provokes actions that deepen the Palestinians' sense of humiliation; and the Palestinians' sense of humiliation provokes reactions that heighten the Israelis' sense of fear—and so on and so forth. When fear and humiliation collide, each becomes stronger.

This dynamic characterizes not only the personal relationships between the two nations but the political one, too. One of the most important goals for the Palestinians is to craft an accord with Israel that does not humiliate them. In contrast, the most important demand for Israelis is to craft an accord with the Palestinians that does not endanger them. And therein lies the problem: the satisfaction of Israel's security needs is bound to injure the Palestinians' *karamah*—their national pride.[6]

Consider one example: most Israelis would probably not support an accord unless the Palestinian state were demilitarized. Moreover, Israelis generally insist that this demilitarization should be enforced, among other steps, by the Israel Defense Forces' continued security control of the Jordan Valley. But this demand is humiliating for the Palestinians: an Israeli military presence on the soil of a Palestinian state would strike a painful blow to its sovereignty and perpetuate the prevailing sense of occupation and humiliation.

Yet both sides have right on their side. For Israelis, a military presence in the Jordan Valley is a necessity on which they cannot compromise; for Palestinians, that military presence is a national humiliation to which they cannot possibly agree.[7]

One further example. Most Israelis would probably reject an accord that closed Palestine's airspace to the Israeli Air Force. The reasons are straightforward: only through freedom of the skies could Israel supervise Palestine's demilitarization, hold necessary training exercises, and ensure the security of its own skies. But there could be no greater humiliation for the Palestinians than to have Israeli jets flying above their heads on a daily basis.[8] Yet again, both sides are right. The same steps that would allay the Israelis' sense of fear would also exacerbate the Palestinians' sense of humiliation.

This is a zero-sum game between one nation's national honor and another's national security. As a result, any agreement that would satisfy Israel's security needs would be perceived as one that perpetuated Israel's control over the Palestinians and therefore humiliated them. Conversely, any agreement that would be acceptable to the Palestinians would be perceived as one that weakened Israel and exposed it to intolerable security threats. When fear and humiliation collide, any possibility for political agreement goes out the window.

Israelis' fear of the Palestinians is a result of decades of conflict, in which at least three generations of Israelis have been exposed to terrorism.[9] If the purpose of terrorism is to sow fear throughout an entire society, then Palestinian terrorism has been a great success. Israelis are afraid. But their fear has deeper roots than the current situation. It is a result not just of Palestinian terrorism but of centuries of Jewish history as well.

The history of the Jews is a history of persecution. In the Jews' collective memory, the past consists of a long and never-ending series of expulsions and pogroms.[10] The belief that "in every generation they rise up to destroy us," repeated at every Passover Seder, has been seared into the depths of the Jewish consciousness. Palestinian terrorism did not create this Israeli fear—it activated an older, Jewish fear in the Israelis' subconscious.

The Palestinians' sense of humiliation has been shaped by decades of Israel's military control over the civilian population of the territories.[11] But this humiliation was not born in 1967. Just as the Israelis' fear has a Jewish history, the Palestinians' sense of humiliation has a Muslim history.

For centuries, the Islamic civilization was the most developed civilization on earth. It was a leader of scientific progress and the source of paradigm-shifting breakthroughs in mathematics, philosophy, and art. It gave birth to some of the greatest astronomers, poets, and thinkers of the day. Islamic civilization was an inspiration for all other faiths, including Judaism. Maimonides, for example, blazed a new path in Jewish philosophy with inspiration from Muslim thinkers, mainly Avicenna and al-Farabi. Some of the great intellectual breakthroughs of the Christian world, such as in the works of Thomas Aquinas, also drew inspiration from Muslim thinkers. Islamic philosophy shone light around the world, while thinkers in Europe—the domain of Christendom—remained largely isolated. The advances of Islamic civilization only emphasized the relative stasis of the Christian world.[12]

European civilizations began to change in the fourteenth century, as thinkers and statesmen began to question church orthodoxy and power. With the Renaissance, and into modern times, Europeans began thinking critically and generating new ideas, sparking political and technological revolutions that transformed the world. No such revolutions occurred in the Islamic world. When European states began to rise, Islamic civilization began to sink: its critical thinking was silenced, its great intellectual life extinguished, and its power diminished. Eventually, the Europeans managed to turn disparities of culture into disparities of power, and they colonized and seized control of the Islamic world.[13]

This painful historic reversal for Islam is the root of the sense of humiliation felt by many Muslims around the world. Their glorious and mighty empire was transformed into something weak and atrophied; and this transition created a powerful sense of offense within the Muslim psyche.[14] This psychological baggage affects the Palestinians' struggle against Israel. Palestinians perceive Israelis as Western invaders who unjustly implanted themselves in the world of Islam. The success of Zionism is a painful and living reminder to Muslims of their ongoing humiliation at the hands of Western civilization.

In sum, just as Palestinian terrorism is not the cause of the Israelis' fear but rather amplifies an older, Jewish fear, Israel's actions today are not the cause of the Palestinians' sense of humiliation but amplify a broader humiliation shared by the Muslim world at large.[15]

Where does this leave the two sides? The emotional attachment of both to their respective positions on the conflict obstructs honest conversation about that conflict. But dialogue about the conflict is not the only victim of their emotional engagement—so is the conflict itself. Ancient Jewish feelings are colliding with ancient Muslim feelings and preventing any possibility of ending the conflict. The conflict has psychological depth, and the psychological depth has historical depth. The whole of both Jewish and Muslim histories are bound up in the conflict, fated to collide with each other. The jubilee year of the Six-Day War offers Israelis an opportunity to renew their thinking about the conflict— and one important innovation they must adopt is to stop thinking in dichotomies and start thinking in degrees.

FROM THINKING IN DICHOTOMIES
TO THINKING IN DEGREES

Jewish religious thought has undergone a transformation in the modern age. Jewish tradition contains a hierarchy of commandments: some are of great importance, others less so. Some commandments are rooted in the Torah itself (these are called *d'oraita*), some are based on the teachings of the sages (*d'rabanan*), and some are technically not commandments at all but customs.

Ultra-Orthodox Jewry collapsed this hierarchy in the nineteenth century. Suddenly, all commandments became equally binding. "For us, the Jewish people," wrote Rabbi Akiva Schlesinger, "the whole *Shulchan Aruch* [code of Jewish law] is equivalent to the Ten Commandments, and every Jewish custom is equivalent to the Ten Commandments as well."[16] Rabbis ordered their congregations to observe mere customs as if they were explicit biblical commandments. They conflated the trivial with the supreme, eliminated all nuance in Jewish religious law, and painted an entire rich and diverse heritage in a single shade.

Not only did religious thought become dichotomous; so did political thought. Just as ultra-Orthodox law eliminated the spectrum of commands and offenses and made everything equally grave, Jewish politics eliminated the spectrum of issues and solutions and made everything equally grave as well. Both left and right translated religious language—the distinctions between pure and impure, sacred and profane—into political language, distinguishing between darkness and enlightenment, patriotism and treason.

Israeli political thought has become binary over the past fifty years: Israel is either an occupying power or a moral society; it is either in conflict or at peace; it is either settling the land or betraying its identity and values. This is the right moment to ask: What will happen if Israelis adjust the way they think about politics? What will happen if they stop seeing politics through ultra-Orthodox eyes and start seeing it through non-dichotomous eyes instead? Such a change would permit them to ask entirely new questions. Instead of asking how to end the conflict, Israelis could ask how to limit it. Instead of asking how to end the occupation, they could ask how to minimize it.

Most importantly, Israelis could reform their attitudes toward peace itself. Israelis are used to talking about peace as something that will "break out" one day. They are inclined to believe that peace is a major, transformational event that will "happen" and change the very foundations of reality. But perhaps peace too requires Israelis to think in terms of degrees. Doing so, they might discover that the world already contains a certain degree of peace, and that Israel's mission is to create more of it.

The Talmud says that Torah scholars "increase peace in the world"—they do not *bring* peace.[17] They increase it through their actions and their studies. Instead of asking how to bring peace, therefore, Israelis must ask what they can do to *increase* it.

All ideas have their own stories, and in this book I shall try to tell the stories of the major political ideas in Israel. These ideas have roots deep in Zionist thought and have become full-fledged political ideologies over the years, colliding with each other with catastrophic power. This clash of ideas has shaken Israeli society to its core, which is why I shall describe them in such bold and dramatic terms. Readers who prefer more reserved formulations are invited to consult the sources listed in the notes.

The debate tearing Israel apart is not based on ideas alone. Other factors are also responsible for widening this rift and preventing Israelis from listening to one another. The debate is fueled by ethnic divisions, class conflict, and even personal political interests. None of these will receive comprehensive treatment in the following discussion. This journey is first and foremost intellectual.

The ideas of Ze'ev Jabotinsky, Rav Kook, Karl Marx, David Ben-Gurion, and others generated the deep undercurrents of modern Israeli politics. In Part I, I discuss the philosophy behind the politics.[18] In Part II, I move from the political thought underlying this discourse to the specific arguments it generates. Throughout I delve into the political arguments in Israel, listening with respect and empathy to the cases made by the different sides over the past fifty years.[19]

The first two parts form the heart of this book. My hope is that my analysis of ideas on the one hand and arguments on the other will give readers a more vivid understanding of the debate that has been rocking Israel ever since the Six-Day War. In Part III, I outline the features of the type of pragmatic mode of thinking that might help alter Israelis' unwillingness to listen to one another.

While researching this book, I discovered that every side in Israel's political debate harbors an unspoken desire to be understood. But healing Israel's national conversation will require Israelis to supplement this wish with a further wish to *understand* as well. Rarely do people possess such a desire, but one person who succeeded was my good friend Sari Rubinstein, who passed away while I was writing this book. Sari possessed an intimate understanding of people, and succeeded in her lifetime in increasing peace in the world. This book is dedicated to her with love and deepest longing.

PART I POLITICAL IDEOLOGIES IN CRISIS

When I see a person walking among us who has answered all his questions and contradictions . . . I wonder whether he is living on another planet, outside our world of tears and vicissitudes, of torments and stolen hopes. . . . As for me, I prefer a mind confused, erratic, and restless over a mind without trouble that is silent about the truths it holds dear.

—Berl Katznelson

INTRODUCTION

Right and Left—A Tale of Two Shifts

The more right-wing Israelis are, the more religious they are; and the more religious they are, the more right-wing they are. This is of course a generalization that does not always hold true, but in Israel today an almost direct correlation exists between being right-wing and being religious.

Things were not always this way. None of the founding fathers of Religious Zionism treated sovereignty over the whole Land of Israel as sacrosanct. Rabbi Yaakov Reines, who founded Religious Zionism in its political form, supported the Uganda Plan—the proposal by the British Empire in the early twentieth century to create a national home for the Jews in eastern Africa. The founder of the movement that would vigorously reject relinquishing parts of the Land of Israel was himself willing to concede the entire land.[1]

Later, the minister representing the National Religious Party, Haim-Moshe Shapira, strongly objected to Israel's launching the Six-Day War. The campaign to restore the people of Israel to their ancient biblical heartland and to the Old City of Jerusalem was waged despite the opposition of the party of the religious nationalists.[2] Anyone who looks at Religious Zionism today will surely be surprised that Rabbi Reines proposed conceding the Holy Land and that Minister Shapira opposed liberating the Old City.

Just as Religious Zionism was not right-wing at its inception, the Israeli right was not predominantly religious at its inception either. The founding father of the Israeli right, Ze'ev Jabotinsky, was the least religious of any of the Zionist leaders of the early twentieth century. Born and raised in the cosmopolitan city of Odessa, Jabotinsky was reared in an intellectual environment that was not in the least religious.[3] Unlike most of the Zionist leaders on the left, who were raised in religious homes and preserved a nostalgic if ambivalent relationship with Jewish tradition their entire lives, Jabotinsky grew up as a secularist, and his attachment to the tradition was weak. The fact that Zionism's least religious leader was also its most right-wing might also appear surprising to today's generation.

The nature of Religious Zionism changed in the years after the Six-Day War, and so did the nature of the secular right. Religious Zionism moved farther to the right during the 1970s; in parallel, the secular right began to weaken until it finally became incorporated into Religious Zionism. This is how one of the most influential ideological forces in Israeli history, the religious right, was born.

Not only did the right undergo a transformational change; so did the left. The Israeli left did not originally focus on peace. The left's passion for many years after its inception was social rather than political. The ultimate goal of the left was to forge solidarity between workers, not peace between nations. The leaders of the historical labor movement—David Ben-Gurion, Moshe Dayan, and Golda Meir—were for years extremely skeptical of the possibility of reaching a lasting peace with the Arabs. They consistently distanced themselves from political initiatives that purported to eliminate the hostility between the two peoples. But the Israeli left underwent a major shift in the years after the Six-Day War. Its leaders replaced socialism with peace as the object of their passion and the pinnacle of their dreams.

These parallel processes occurred almost simultaneously. While the right evolved to become less secular and liberal, and more religious and messianic, the left evolved from a social movement into a diplomatic one. The new left and the new right collided with tremendous force, sparking the ideological conflict that unfolded after the Six-Day War. In the following chapters, I tell the story of these new ideas.

1 THE RIGHT'S IDEOLOGICAL SHIFT

JABOTINSKY'S THREE PROPHETIC VISIONS

Ze'ev Jabotinsky was a doom-monger. Wherever he looked, he saw nothing but grave threats to the Jewish people looming. He warned against the treachery of the British, the aggression of the Arabs, and the coming annihilation of the Jews in Europe, a catastrophe he predicted. History painfully proved that his visions became realities. Jabotinsky was the man who was almost always right.

During World War I, the British committed themselves to helping the Jewish people establish a national home in the Land of Israel. This commitment, made in writing in the famous letter of 2 November 1917 known as the Balfour Declaration, formed the basis of the mandate that defined Britain's obligation to the Jews and inspired tremendous optimism among many Zionists.

But Jabotinsky did not succumb to this intoxicating spirit of optimism. He was certain that the British would break their promise. He believed that without active political involvement by the Zionists, the British would turn their backs on the Jews in favor of an alternative alliance with the Arabs.[1] Over the years, the British did indeed begin to back away from their commitment to the Jewish people. By the time Britain published the infamous White Paper in 1939, limiting Jewish migration to Palestine and rejecting the idea of partitioning Palestine, it had become clear that Britain no longer felt bound by the Balfour Declaration. On the eve of World War II, the British finally abandoned the commitments made during World War I.

As the Nazis were gaining power in Germany in the 1930s, Jabotinsky warned repeatedly of a terrible catastrophe that would soon befall the Jews of Europe: "We are living on the brink of the abyss, the eve of a final disaster in the global ghetto."[2] He tried to shake the Zionist movement out of its complacency, and urged the Zionists to push for the migration of the Jews of Europe to Palestine. The man who correctly predicted the Jews' betrayal at the hands of the British also correctly predicted their annihilation at the hands of the Germans.[3]

Jabotinsky was also right about the Arabs. Contrary to widespread opinion among Zionists, Jabotinsky foresaw that mass immigration to Palestine by the Jews would provoke mass resistance in Palestine from the Arabs. Jabotinsky wrote that the anti-Jewish Jaffa riots of 1921 were not an exception to the norm but were now the norm.[4] The Zionist movement was unwittingly marching toward a violent confrontation with the Arab national movement. Some Zionists believed that the Arabs would not object to Zionism because they were certain to benefit from it.[5] Jabotinsky saw this position as patronizing:

> This childish fantasy of our "Arabophiles" is rooted in a kind of prejudiced contempt for the Arab people, in a kind of to-

tally groundless perception of this race, which sees it as a corrupt mob that would surrender its homeland for a good railway system. There is no justification for this perception. It may be possible to bribe individual Arabs, and to do so often. But from this it does not follow that the Arabs of the Land of Israel as a collective will sell their fanatical sense of patriotism, which even the Papuans refuse to sell. Every nation will wage a struggle against settlers so long as it has even a glimmer of hope to be rid of the danger of their settling the land. This is what the Arabs of the Land of Israel have done, and this is what they will continue to do.[6]

Zionist patriots needed to understand that the Arabs were also patriots, believed Jabotinsky.[7] They would not sell their right to nationhood for a mere improvement in their quality of life. Jabotinsky taught that it is precisely the Zionist who respects the Arabs who should prepare for war with them.[8]

Jabotinsky foresaw the coming treachery of the British, the impending destruction by the Germans, and the inevitable clash with the Arabs. He was a suspicious man and a pessimist, and, tragically, he was almost always right.

LIBERAL AND SKEPTICAL POLITICAL THOUGHT

"It was a wise philosopher," Jabotinsky once wrote, "who said, *Homo homini lupus*. Man behaves worse than a wolf toward a fellow man, and this cannot be remedied for many years— neither by political reform, nor by the grace of culture, nor even by the bitter experience of life. A fool is he who believes his neighbor, no matter how good and friendly the neighbor might be."[9] Jabotinsky was convinced that political reform could never repair human nature. It was dangerously naive, he thought, to believe that a political society could ever be constructed that would do away with human evil. "He who places his faith in justice is a fool, for justice serves only those who forcefully and stubbornly demand it. When I am accused of promoting separatism, of a lack of trust, and of other such expressions that offend sensitive ears, I wish to answer as I must: Guilty as charged! I support this all, and shall continue to do so. Because separatism, a lack of trust, keeping one's guard and a truncheon in one's hand—this is the only way to hold one's ground in this faithless den of wolves."[10]

Jabotinsky's suspicion of the British, Germans, and Arabs was not incidental. It was rooted in a broader worldview that was skeptical of human beings in general.[11] People, he believed, harbor violent impulses that cannot be eliminated by mere social arrangements. Because of this, they need to preserve the option of war even in times of peace. This is classical right-wing thought: suspicion of human nature generates suspicion in politics, which in turn encourages hyper-defensiveness, self-segregation, and militarism—all of which can be found in Jabotinsky's agenda.[12] But there were further steps in Jabotinsky's thought, rooted not in suspicion of human nature but in faith in the supreme status of the individual.

Jabotinsky proclaimed the majesty of the individual: whereas in dictatorships a single person governs the many, Jabotinsky declared that the individual must always govern him- or herself.[13] The individual is a rich and complex being, destined to be free. Nobody may stop a person from fulfilling his or her full potential, or impinge on an individual's freedom of speech. A free society is one in which every individual may express that individuality in all its richness. The individual must never be subordinate to a king. The individual *is* a king: "In the beginning, God created the individual. Each individual is a king unto himself, with equal value to his neighbor—even the wicked are kings in their own right. Better that the individual sin against society than that society sin against the individual. Society was created for the sake of the individual."[14]

Here, Jabotinsky forcefully expresses a liberal worldview. The individual was not born to serve society; society was born to serve the individual.[15] The individual does not belong to the state; the state belongs to the individual. Anyone who maintains such a belief could well end up endorsing anarchism: since every form of government necessarily limits individual freedom, the path to true liberation must lie in abolishing government altogether. And indeed, Jabotinsky's ideal world was one of anarchy. He dreamt of a world without government, in which every single person could be a ruler unto himself or herself. "The vision of the messianic era in the end of days is a paradise of the individual," he wrote, "a glorious anarchy, a game of twists and turns between the forces of the individual without law and without limitation."[16]

This principle of the supremacy of the individual entails the liberal principle of limiting the power of the majority.[17] This is the foundation of the liberal character of Jabotinsky's Zionism. A Jewish state would have a Jewish majority, but its Christian and Muslim minorities would also be kings unto themselves. "If we have a Jewish majority in this land, we will first and foremost establish a regime of complete, total, and perfect equality of rights, without a single exception. Whether one is a Jew, an Arab, an Armenian, or a German matters not at all to the law—every path must be open to every citizen."[18]

When Jabotinsky spoke of "complete, total, and perfect" equality of rights, he meant it. He imagined the Arabs as partners in the running of the country and in the joint leadership of the government. "In every cabinet in which a Jew serves as prime minister," he wrote, "the post of deputy prime minister shall be offered to an Arab—and vice versa."[19]

Jabotinsky blended a cautious worldview with a liberal political philosophy. He was deeply suspicious of the rivals and enemies of the Jewish people, but he demanded that Jews exhibit immense sensitivity to the minorities living among them. This combination is rare, and barely exists in the modern day.

What became of the liberal right? Why did Jabotinsky's blend of great suspicion toward enemies with great sensitivity toward minorities disappear? Before we confront this issue, we need to delve into it more deeply. For there is an additional tension in Jabotinsky's thinking, no less mysterious. Not only did he reconcile a belief in individual liberty with suspicion of the individual—he also believed in Zionism as the pursuit of both a Greater Israel and international diplomacy.

THE BORDERS OF THE PROMISED LAND

Jabotinsky maintained that the Zionist movement was too passive and pacifist. He called for a vigorous and active style of political Zionism, one that would demand that the international community permit the creation of a stable Jewish majority throughout the entire Land of Israel. The territory he was referring to included both banks of the Jordan River. And from what source did Jabotinsky derive his position on the expansive borders to be demanded from the international community? From none other than the international community itself.

When the allied powers decided to grant Palestine to Britain in April 1921 at the San Remo Conference—convened to apportion territories of the former Ottoman Empire—the British committed themselves, as the mandate stipulated, to advancing the establishment of a national home for the Jewish people. The borders of Palestine at the time included both banks of the Jordan River. The mandate was confirmed by the League of Nations in July 1922, and thereby became the official commitment of the international community to the Jewish people. Given this, Jabotinsky argued that the borders that the Zionists must demand from the international community were not drawn in the Bible but in international treaties.[20] The Jews received the land from an international covenant at San Remo, not from a covenant with God at Mount Sinai. The authority that determined the borders of the Land of Israel was not divine revelation but international consensus.[21]

It might seem strange to modern observers, but the Promised Land of the time was indeed a promised land—but it was promised not by God but by men. Nowadays, those who covet a Greater Israel and oppose territorial compromise are largely uninterested in the concerns of the international community. But Jabotinsky's territorial maximalism was founded on the opposite belief. Jabotinsky did not espouse indifference to the international community, but a demand that its members fulfill their promise.[22]

For Jabotinsky, these contradictions complemented one another. He was suspicious of foreign powers on the outside and supportive of human rights on the inside. He advocated a Zionism that pursued both the creation of a Greater Israel and international diplomacy. In his eyes, these goals could best be pursued in tandem. Jabotinsky was a right-winger who believed in diplomacy, territorial maximalism, and liberalism. The apparent contradictions that merged effortlessly in Jabotinsky's agile and complex mind, however, fell apart in the generations that followed.

THE FRACTURING OF THE REVISIONIST WORLDVIEW

Menachem Begin succeeded Jabotinsky as the leader of the Zionist right and inherited his maximalism.[23] He declared again and again that the Land of Israel spanned both banks of the Jordan.[24] Begin also inherited Jabotinsky's liberalism: it was Begin who demanded that the Mapai (Workers Party) government lift the martial law it had imposed on Israeli Arabs during the 1950s and 1960s following the War of Independence. It was Begin who insisted that the Knesset ratify a constitution in order to limit the government and protect individual rights.[25]

This situation, too, is likely to confound modern observers: it was the left whose political order threatened individual rights, while the right fought for limited government and the protection of individual liberties. The same right wing that demanded the creation of a Greater Israel also demanded full civil rights for the inhabitants of that Greater Israel.[26] The fragile connection between liberalism and maximalism passed from Jabotinsky to Begin, but it did not survive the transition from Begin to his successors. This viewpoint fractured within the ranks of the third generation of Revisionist Zionists.

The third generation of the Israeli right includes many of the sons and daughters of the country's founding generation, members of the paramilitary Irgun and its offshoot the Lehi. The former deputy prime minister Dan Meridor, for instance, is the son of the Irgun commander Eliyahu Meridor. The former foreign minister Tzipi Livni is the daughter of the Irgun operations officer Eitan Livni. The communications minister Tzachi Hanegbi is the son of the Lehi spokeswoman Geula Cohen. The former agriculture minister Yair Shamir is the son of Yitzhak Shamir, commander of the Lehi and later prime minister.

This list also includes the former culture minister Limor Livnat, the former public security minister Uzi Landau, the former health minister Roni Milo, the former housing minister Ze'ev Boim, and the former prime minister Ehud Olmert, as well as President Reuven Rivlin and Prime Minister Benjamin Netanyahu. These right-wing leaders and others, some of the most famous figures in Israel's third political generation, are the sons and daughters of the Revisionist fighters and activists from before the state's establishment.[27] This group of dynastic leaders, dubbed "the princes" by the journalist Eitan Haber, is almost without parallel in world political history.[28] Ironically, however, these biological heirs were not always faithful intellectual heirs.

Many of the princes—including Tzipi Livni, Dan Meridor, Ehud Olmert, Roni Milo, and, if we take him at his word, Benjamin Netanyahu—have renounced their initial hope for Israeli sovereignty over the entire Land of Israel and publicly supported the partition of the land into two states. Some of the princes remained faithful to their parents' legacies, but for the most part they charted a new course.[29] The princes honored their parents but did not follow their path. Ironically, the movement that preserved more continuity than any other failed to preserve the continuity of its ideas.

This ideological shift was largely a result of new circumstances. The dream of a Greater Israel suffered a serious blow in the First Intifada, the Arab uprising that began in December 1987. When masses of Palestinian children took to the streets to rain rocks and Molotov cocktails on Israeli soldiers and settlers, Israelis suffered a major trauma. Israeli citizens were called up for stints of reserve duty lasting forty days at a time, but they were not handed weapons to guard the country's borders from a foreign invasion. Instead, they received clubs to patrol civilian neighborhoods and found themselves chasing children who had scribbled graffiti or waved Palestinian flags.

Reservists returned home deeply scarred. They had enlisted to fight, not to police; to protect their own people, not to rule over another. As time went on, Israeli citizens became increasingly aware of how problematic it was to impose military rule on a civilian population. This realization spread across Israeli society and was internalized by the Israeli right. The marriage between liberalism and territorial maximalism suddenly appeared both forced and unsustainable.

The so-called "demographic problem" began to enter Israelis' consciousness at the end of the 1980s.[30] The intifada had increased Israelis' awareness of both the existence of the Palestinian civilian population and the danger it posed to the survival of a Jewish majority in the Land of Israel. At the heart of the demographic problem is a simple calculation accepted by most experts: the Palestinian population growth rate is higher than the Israeli population growth rate; the day is therefore approaching when most of the inhabitants of the Land of Israel will not be Jews.[31]

So Israelis were compelled to ask, When the Jews become a minority within their own country, will they still have a country of their own? This demographic nightmare has been beaten into the minds of many Israelis and has gravely wounded the liberal wing of the Israeli right. The demographic argument was what persuaded Prime Minister Ariel Sharon, as he said, to pull back Israeli settlements from the Gaza Strip in 2005.[32] The fear of losing a Jewish majority is what propelled Ehud Olmert and Tzipi Livni, as they stated, to enter into intensive and comprehensive negotiations with the Palestinians in 2007 for the partition of the land.[33] And it was this demographic fear, that Israel could eventually become a binational state, that pushed Benjamin Netanyahu—as he explicitly claimed—to make his landmark speech at Bar Ilan University in 2009 outlining the need to establish a demilitarized Palestinian state next to Israel.[34]

Jabotinsky's thought consolidated, as I have noted, two values: territorial maximalism and individual liberalism. But by the third generation of Revisionist Zionists, the understanding that it was impossible to pursue both principles in tandem had become widespread. In practice, Revisionism had already begun to contract to one of its constituent parts—territorial maximalism—in Jabotinsky's day. But today, the opposite process is happening. In the past, activists and thinkers relinquished liberalism in favor of territorial maximalism: the right-wing figures Israel Eldad, Abba Ahimeir, and Uri Zvi Greenberg clung to an extremely maximalist Zionist worldview but rejected liberal tendencies.[35] The nov-elty of the third generation of Revisionist Zionists is not that its adherents broke away from the founding principle of liberalism but that they retained nothing but that founding principle.

Whereas Eldad and Ahimeir abandoned liberalism and were left only with their territorial maximalism, Livni and Meridor abandoned territorial maximalism and were left only with their liberalism.

The demographic considerations had not been alien to Ja-botinsky's philosophy—they were an integral part of it.[36] Jabot-insky talked numbers. He repeatedly declared, "The purpose of Zionism can be summarized in just one sentence: the creation of a Jewish majority in the Land of Israel."[37] In another context, Jabotinsky said, "We're running a marathon against the Arabs: whichever population grows more quickly, wins."[38] For Jabotin-sky, the supreme goal of Zionism was the creation of a Jewish majority in the Land of Israel, for only with a Jewish majority could full human rights be extended to minorities without en-dangering the very essence of Zionism—the sovereignty of the Jewish people.[39]

"If we have a Jewish majority in this land," Jabotinsky wrote, "we will first and foremost establish a regime of complete, total, and perfect equality of rights."[40] Jabotinsky was explicit that the basic condition for comprehensive equality of rights throughout the land was the existence of a Jewish majority there. Given that, the next question must be, What did Jabotinsky's philosophy in-dicate should happen if Jews were *not* a majority? What should Israelis do then?

Jabotinsky had three main ambitions: demographic, territorial, and political. Demographically, he wanted a decisive Jewish majority. Territorially, he wanted this majority to extend over both sides of the River Jordan. Politically, he wanted minorities living within this territory to enjoy full and equal rights. This three-fold aim was achievable in Jabotinsky's day, at least in theory. Millions of Jews lived in Europe; if most of them had immigrated, Palestine would have had a massive Jewish majority. But the extermination of European Jewry changed Jewish demographics forever, making it impossible for them to dream any longer of realizing all three ambitions. The way to create a Jewish majority in Jabotinsky's day was to encourage mass immigration— and some Israelis still believe that a majority can be achieved thus, without territorial compromise. But when the princes relinquished the objective of a land united in favor of safeguarding the Jewish majority on a land divided, they compromised on one goal of Jabotinsky's philosophy. They did so, however, in order to realize a different, no less important, goal of that philosophy.

I have laid out with great brevity the story of a big, all-embracing ideology that fractured into its constituent parts. Jabotinsky's philosophy contained tension between principles that conflicted in theory—but when they collided in practice, the strain of liberalism ultimately overpowered the strain of territorial maximalism.

The right splintered, but did not fall apart—it adapted. For a different ideological group had begun to gain dominance on the right, instilling it with new life. This was the messianic religious right. The new right stopped talking about a land promised by the international community and began talking about a land promised by God.[41] In this incarnation, the Jewish people's right to the whole land was based not on an international covenant but on a divine covenant. The secular right was weakened by an ideological crisis, and the religious right was strengthened by an ideological awakening—the result was a revolution that transformed the entire intellectual universe of the Israeli right. The basic impulse of the modern right is no longer liberal; it is messianic.[42]

The transition that created the modern right unfolded in parallel with a major shift that occurred on the Israeli left. This story will be told in the next chapter.

2 THE LEFT'S IDEOLOGICAL SHIFT

For most of its existence, the dominant stream of the Israeli left did not believe in making peace with the Arabs.[1] From the early twentieth century until the 1970s, the labor movement never touted a peace deal as one of its central aims. The left's deep suspicion of the Arab world foreclosed any hope of making peace with the Arabs. The IDF chief of staff, Moshe Dayan, gave voice to the sober attitude of the Mapai generation in his celebrated eulogy for Roi Rotberg, who was killed in 1956 by Palestinian infiltrators from Gaza:

> We are a generation of settlement, and without the steel helmet and the barrel of the cannon we shall neither plant a tree nor build a house. Our children shall not have lives unless we dig shelters, and without a fence of barbed wire and machine guns we shall neither pave a path nor drill for water. . . . Beyond the furrow of that border boils a sea of hatred and vengeance, waiting for the day the quiet dulls our alertness, for the day we heed the conspiring ambassadors of hypocrisy, who call on us to lay down our arms. . . . This is the choice of our lives: to be

ready and armed, strong and uncompromising, or to let the sword drop from our hands—and to be mown down.

Dayan did not change his view after the Six-Day War. He explained in 1969 that the State of Israel would always be perceived as a foreign body in the Middle East: "We are a heart transplant in a region where the other organs do not match the heart and are trying to reject it."[2] At the same time, Shimon Peres, then minister of immigrant absorption—who would later become the great prophet of peace—was also extremely doubtful of the possibility of reaching a peace deal: "Israel is surrounded by Arab states. . . . The Arab purpose is all-absorptive—the destruction of Israel and the annihilation or banishment of her inhabitants. . . . No compromise can satisfy them. It is the Arab goal to abolish Israel, not to change a political situation."[3]

Peace is an illusion, the left argued, and no peace agreement could alleviate the Arab world's implacable hatred of Israel. This deep sense of suspicion found expression in deed as well as in word. In 1971, the government of Golda Meir rejected Egypt's overtures for a diplomatic solution to the conflict between the two nations.[4]

If the left did not believe in peace and did not hope for a peace accord, what was its ideology? Until it made its historic shift, the left concerned itself with crafting not diplomatic initiatives but a model socialist society.

TWO CONCEPTIONS OF TIME

"The history of all hitherto existing societies is the history of class struggles," determined Karl Marx.[5] In other words, the real drama driving history forward is class war. Throughout human history, every ruling class has oppressed and exploited those in its power while deploying alluring ideologies to disguise that exploitation. But this history of injustice, said Marx, is marching toward its certain demise. Workers will inevitably rise up in open rebellion against capitalism, will destroy the ruling unjust society, and will build an enlightened society atop its ruins, free of oppression and exploitation.

This conception of time was common to socialists worldwide. The past was dark—a never-ending tale of the oppression of the working class—whereas the future, when equality and solidarity between workers would prevail, would be bright. The present was but a difficult and challenging period of transition between the dark past and a bright future.

For the Zionist left, the purpose of Zionism was to deliver the Jews from a past of exploitation into a future of solidarity. The present was difficult, they rationalized, because all transitional periods are difficult. But they were certain that this painful reality would give rise to a new era of Hebrew brotherhood between workers, a spirit that would inspire the whole of humanity.

The left's intellectual focus underwent a major shift in the 1970s. Leftists began to move away from the dream of a model socialist society, replacing it with the dream of peace. Solidarity between nations was to take the place of solidarity between workers. The dream of peace succeeded socialism, therefore, while also inheriting its optimism.

This dream was, like the socialist dream, rooted in a clear conception of time. Israel's history can be divided, in the left's revised worldview, into two parts: before the Six-Day War, Israel was an ethical democracy whose citizens dreamt of building a model society; since the war it has become an ethnical occupier, corrupt by definition. The only way forward, therefore, is for the State of Israel to reach a peace agreement with the Arab world.

So while the worldview of the Israeli left has evolved, the left's conception of time has remained static. The past is rooted in sin, the future in redemption. History is not the story of the oppression of the workers but the story of the occupation of the Palestinians. The future demands not solidarity between workers but peace between peoples. And the present is not defined by a struggle for social revolution, but by a struggle for an equally revolutionary agreement for peace.[6]

We have witnessed how the right evolved from liberalism to messianism. But how did the left evolve from socialism to diplomacy?

THE RISE AND FALL OF SOCIALIST ZIONISM

Many of the founders of Zionism were immigrants from Russia who landed on the shores of Palestine invigorated by the revolutionary spirit of socialism. Unlike their Russian comrades, however, these early Zionists had chosen not to foment revolution but to build their model socialist society in the Land of Israel. Not all Zionists at the time were socialists. But among the different streams of Zionism, it was the one that fused itself with socialism that most profoundly shaped Israeli society at its birth. The socialist Zionists led the Yishuv, the pre-state Jewish community; they led the nascent State of Israel; and they continued to lead the Zionist movement well into the 1970s. Many of them believed that the Israel of the future would not only be a model socialist society; it would also be a model to be emulated by the whole of humanity.

It became clear over time that the future would not deliver the longed-for socialist redemption—history was about to destroy it. The Israeli left suffered a serious blow during the Cold War. The contest between superpowers was also a contest between ideologies, between capitalism and socialism. The Soviet Union was an early supporter of the Jewish state, having voted in favor of its establishment in the U.N. Partition Plan of 29 November 1947. The Soviets even helped Israel secure arms during the 1948 War of Independence. But in the 1950s, the Communist regime in Moscow shifted to the support of Israel's enemies.

It soon became undeniably clear that the Soviet Union was not only anti-Israel but institutionally anti-Semitic. Millions of oppressed Jews were suddenly locked behind the Soviet Union's iron gates. Later, when Stalin's horrific crimes were exposed in 1956, it became plain that the Soviet regime was not just anti-Israel and anti-Semitic but anti-humanity as well.

The more objectionable the Soviet Union appeared, the more the magnetic power of its ideas waned. When Israel began to move away from socialism, the government also began to cultivate an alliance with the United States. As the United States became the predominant power in the West, it also became Israel's firmest supporter. And as the Jews of America thrived and prospered, their coreligionists in the Soviet Union continued to struggle under oppression. In time, the American brand of capitalism spread around the world, the Israeli economy began the process of privatization, and the Israeli education system started an accelerated program of Americanization.[7]

Eventually, communism collapsed in the Soviet Union, and Communist regimes were brought down around the world. In Israel, the surviving enclaves of communism—the collective communities of the kibbutz movement—were almost all privatized. Israel had started out under the heavy cultural influence of Russia, but moved decisively into the cultural sphere of the United States.

In the years after the new millennium, campaigns for social change have been revived around Israel. Their seminal moment was the summer of 2011, when thousands of Israelis left their homes and encamped in tents in Tel Aviv. Hundreds of thousands of Israelis took to the streets to march in protest. Countless citizens participated in rowdy demonstrations, shouting in unison, "The nation demands social justice!"

Was this demand for social justice a call to revive Zionism in its socialist incarnation? Not quite. For the protesters of the summer of 2011, social justice was to be achieved through urgent action to reduce the cost of housing, lower sales taxes, and cut prices by breaking up monopolies and injecting greater competition into the Israeli market. The issue most commonly identified in Israel today as a "social" issue is the cost of living. This is not a call to restore socialist Zionism; ironically, it is proof of the victory of Western capitalism. The socialist Zionism of the early twentieth century was concerned with the rights of the worker; the social campaigns of the twenty-first century focus on the rights of the consumer. Solidarity of workers has been replaced by solidarity of consumers. How ironic that the final nail in the coffin of socialist Zionism was hammered in specifically by the Israeli social justice movement.

FROM SOCIALISM TO PEACE

By the end of the Six-Day War, the borders of Israel had expanded to include the Sinai Peninsula, the Gaza Strip, Judea and Samaria, and the Golan Heights. Israel controlled territories that were once ruled by Egypt, Jordan, and Syria. For the first time, Israel now held strong bargaining cards for negotiating with the Arab world. The Israeli government decided in June 1967 to offer most of these territories back to the Arab states in exchange for a comprehensive peace treaty.[8] The United Nations Security Council declared that this was the deal that could stabilize the Middle East, as expressed in U.N. Resolution 242, which first established the political formula of land for peace. For the first time since Israel's creation and the armistice agreements of 1949, an opportunity had emerged to end the conflict between Israel and its Arab neighbors once and for all.

The Arab world's response to Israel's offer, however, was disappointing. In September 1967, the Arab League convened in Khartoum, Sudan, and announced its Three Noes retort to Israel's peace offering: no peace with Israel, no recognition of Israel, and no negotiations with Israel.

The Arabs first united in rejection of Israel's peace overtures, and a few years later united again in an embrace of war. With impressive coordination and pan-Arab support, Egypt and Syria launched a surprise attack on Israel on the afternoon of Yom Kippur 1973. This heavy war claimed the lives of many Israelis and left countless more wounded. But following the attack, Anwar Sadat, the Egyptian president who had initiated it, broke ranks with the rest of the Arab world and turned his attention to making peace instead.

Israel's response to the Egyptian peace initiative bordered on the ecstatic. Israelis were exultant when Sadat landed in Israel, addressed the Knesset, and extended his hand in peace. The country was as surprised by Egypt's overture of peace as it had been by Egypt's launch of war. The unanticipated attack had destroyed the faith of many Israelis in the leaders of socialist Zionism. The unanticipated peace overture offered an alternative to those socialist ideals—peace.[9]

The peace negotiations between Israel's prime minister, Menachem Begin, and Sadat were not easy, and at one point hit a major crisis. One of the biggest obstacles confronting negotiators was the question of the political status of the Palestinians. Egypt had conditioned peace with Israel on the establishment of a Palestinian state. Israel preferred to keep the peace treaty with Egypt separate from any future agreement relating to the Palestinian residents of the territories. At one point, it looked as though the negotiations were on the verge of collapse because the Begin government insisted that it would never relinquish Judea and Samaria, certainly not as part of a peace treaty with Egypt.[10]

This was the backdrop for the establishment of the Israeli peace movement. It was founded to urge the Begin government to jump over all the hurdles, make all the necessary concessions, and not delay the prospect of peace any further. In other words: Peace Now. The Israeli peace movement differs from most peace movements around the world inasmuch as it was not formed to protest a war but to support an initiative to end a war. In contrast to the concurrent peace movement in the United States, which sprang up in opposition to the Vietnam War, the Israeli peace movement did not emerge out of frustration with an ongoing war but out of hope for a possible future peace.[11]

The peace treaty that was ultimately signed between Israel and Egypt in 1979 gave the new left a fresh impetus and injected it with renewed hope. The peace camp called for Israel's withdrawal from the territories and the establishment of peaceful relations with the Palestinians to pave the way for peace with the entire Arab world. Many Israelis believed that the threat of war could be extinguished and that doing so depended only on Israel's political courage in negotiating with the Arabs.

The first attempts to translate this dream into reality took place in the early 1990s. A public effort was made at the 1991 Madrid Conference, which was cosponsored by the United States and the Soviet Union, and included Israel's neighbors but excluded the Palestinian Liberation Organization (PLO); it was followed by the secret meetings between Israel and the PLO that led to the 1993 Oslo Accords. Slowly, a peace agreement between Israel and the Palestinians began to take shape. The Israeli foreign minister, Shimon Peres—one of Israel's most important and eloquent advocates of peace—published a book in 1993 articulating the latest vision of the new Israeli left: *The New Middle East.*[12] Peres argued that peace with the Palestinians would only be the first stage in a process that would lead to peace with the entire Arab world. This peace would find expression in regional economic cooperation and in the bridging of the divisive gulfs that had kept the various parties apart. In Peres's vision, every inhabitant of the Middle East would enjoy the fruits of such economic cooperation, and the prosperity that peace would bring would also guarantee the stability of that peace.

Peres's grand theory sought to explain how the State of Israel could be transformed, through political and economic change, into an organic part of the Middle East, as well as into an accepted, legitimate country in the eyes of the entire world. The history of the Jews has been a history of their alienation, and of perpetual tensions with the nations of the world. The Oslo Accords were designed not only to change the relationship between Israel and the Palestinians but to change the course of Jewish history. The Jewish people had already ended their long exile from their homeland. The Oslo Accords were supposed to end their exile from the rest of humanity as well.

The story of the Israeli left is of a journey from the pursuit of socialism to the pursuit of peace.[13] The story of the Israeli right is of a journey from liberalism to messianism. These two journeys took place almost in perfect parallel. The 1980s and the 1990s were the years when a mighty clash took place between the new Israeli right and the new Israeli left. The right of "Greater Israel" and the left of "Peace Now" confronted each other with incredible passion and set the public sphere aflame.

But these shifts, too, were only temporary.

A NEW SHIFT

The history of these two ideas—Greater Israel and Peace Now—runs through two intifadas. The First Intifada erupted at the end of 1987 and wounded the secular right. The numbers speak for themselves. In 1987, at the outset of the First Intifada, only 21 percent of Israelis favored the establishment of a Palestinian state.[14] But by 2001, 57 percent of Israelis backed the idea.[15] The popular Arab uprising had led most in Israeli society to conclude that Israel could no longer continue ruling over the Palestinians.

But if the First Intifada injured the Israeli right, the Second Intifada almost completely destroyed the Israeli left. The Second Intifada exploded in September 2000; it involved less popular Arab participation, and it was much more violent than its predecessor. The rioters of the First Intifada were now joined by suicide bombers. The Palestinians did not just throw stones—they blew up buses. The intifada targeted women and children in Tel Aviv and Jerusalem along with soldiers in the territories. This intifada pulverized the left, not simply because of the ferocity of its violence but mainly because of its timing: it came only two months after the Camp David Summit.

At the Camp David Summit of July 2000, Israeli Prime Minister Ehud Barak made Palestinian Authority Chairman Yasser Arafat an offer that U.S. President Bill Clinton described as the best one that Arafat could hope to receive from an Israeli prime minister. The offer shattered many of Israel's myths and slaughtered even more of its sacred cows. It included a withdrawal from nearly all the territories conquered in the Six-Day War, the division of Jerusalem between Israel and the Palestinians, and a compromise over the Temple Mount. Arafat refused the offer, without presenting a counteroffer of his own.[16] The Palestinians' final response came two months later in the form of a lethal wave of suicide bombers.[17]

As the great majority of Israelis understood it, the Second Intifada did not break out *because* of the occupation; it broke out after Israel offered to *end* the occupation.[18] The argument that the occupation was the cause of the Israeli-Palestinian conflict was soon discredited, as the conflict had escalated at precisely the time Israel proposed ending it. In the words of the Israeli journalist Ari Shavit, expressing the left's frustration in a 2014 article, "Exactly 14 years ago, Israel's most generous peace offer led to the worst terror attack on Israel."[19]

The Second Intifada pulverized the Israeli left. The notion that peace was waiting around the corner and that the path would be paved with Israeli concessions looked more far-fetched than ever. The movement born during the Camp David Accords with Egypt died after the Camp David Summit with the Palestinians.

The vision of peace holds a central place in the history of Israel's political ideas. As we have seen, peace succeeded socialism as the leading ideal of the left, thereby rescuing the Israeli left from a potential intellectual crisis. But when the idea of peace collapsed, no other optimistic idea arose to take its place. The intellectual crisis that should have arisen after the collapse of socialism came about after the collapse of peace initiatives instead.

TWO DREAMS VERSUS TWO INTIFADAS

The First Intifada shattered the secular right, while the Second Intifada shattered the Zionist left.[20] So where does Israeli society stand now that it has survived two violent intifadas? Here too, the numbers speak for themselves. Over 70 percent of Israelis have no desire to rule over the Palestinians, but a similar proportion have no faith in the possibility of reaching a peace agreement with them.[21] This is the trap that we shall confront later: the survivors of two intifadas cannot imagine the land remaining united, nor can they imagine it remaining at peace.

At the arrival of the new millennium, Israel entered a post-ideological era. The secular right took a blow when its liberalism defeated its maximalism. The Zionist left collapsed when the Second Intifada trounced its hope of peace. When these ideas had been abandoned, only one ideology still stood: the Zionism of the religious right. It drew its most powerful inspiration at the moment when its rivals lost theirs.

3 RELIGIOUS ZIONISM AND THE MESSIANIC SHIFT

THE METAMORPHOSIS OF RELIGIOUS ZIONISM

Religious Zionism has not always been the purview of the right. The great shift in Religious Zionism took place in the 1970s but was rooted in the events of June 1967.[1] In six days of war, the world of the Religious Zionists was created anew. The war was interpreted as nothing less than a biblical drama. Not only was Israel's victory understood as a miracle on a biblical scale; it had restored the Jews to their ancient biblical heartland. After the war, Israeli history began to look increasingly divine. God, it seemed, had returned to history.

The religious excitement inspiring the scions of Religious Zionism now found expression in a religious language, as expounded in the messianic philosophy of Rabbi Abraham Isaac Kook, also known as HaRav—*the* rabbi. Rabbi Kook's philosophy, further developed by his son Rabbi Zvi Yehuda Kook, had been confined for years to the periphery of the Religious Zionist movement. It quickly became the movement's all but official philosophy.

Rabbi Zvi Yehuda Kook interpreted the historic events of 1967 as the realization of various stages in God's messianic plan. To his mind, the extension of Jewish sovereignty over biblical soil was the strongest possible indication that the Jews were already in the advanced stages of the Redemption. Withdrawal from any part of the Land of Israel, therefore, would be an act of sabotage against progress toward the Redemption. For Religious Zionists, the struggle against an Israeli withdrawal was not just a fight over real estate but a fight for the onward march of history toward the messianic era.

The messianic shift of Religious Zionism occurred almost simultaneously with the ideological crisis of the secular right. As a result, the Religious Zionist movement became a dominant component of the political universe of the right, and the messianic narrative became its dominant narrative.

Thus was revolutionized the central idea of the Israeli right. At the inception of the Israeli right, "Greater Israel" was understood as the land promised by the international community, based on the Jews' deep historical roots and indigeneity in that land; by the end of the twentieth century, it was understood as the land promised by God. At its inception, the right's dominant faction placed its emphasis on human rights; by the end of the twentieth century, the right's dominant faction placed its emphasis on the Redemption. These shifts not only altered the right; they strengthened it. Once adherents experienced the fight for Greater Israel as a fight for redemption, they gained almost unstoppable momentum.

THE THEOLOGICAL FOUNDATIONS
OF THE RELIGIOUS RIGHT

Rabbi Kook the elder was an interpreter of both books and events. Mysticism is a method of interpreting sacred texts that teases out the layers hidden between the lines. All texts have a literal meaning, but deep down they also conceal secrets. Likewise, a mystical interpretation of history is a search for layers of meaning within the past that remain invisible to the naked eye. Rabbi Kook believed that secular Zionism had a "literal meaning" but that it also enshrouded a profound secret at its core. Secular Zionism, he argued, was also a messianic movement—and the secular Jews at its head were fundamentally religious without knowing it.

This mystical historiography aroused little interest or acceptance during Rabbi Kook's lifetime or in the generation that followed. But it enjoyed a dramatic revival after Israel's stunning victory in the Six-Day War.[2] In the 1970s, this interpretation —repackaged by its founder's son Rabbi Zvi Yehuda Kook— completely transformed the face of Religious Zionism.[3]

Many of the biblical prophets, noted Rabbi Zvi Yehuda, proclaimed the same vision: the Jewish people's destiny was to be gathered in from Exile and restored to their Promised Land. The rebirth of the Jewish state and the waves of Jewish immigration around the world, the miraculous Six-Day War, and the settlement of biblical soil—none of these events could be understood as anything but the fulfillment of the ancient prophecies. For Rabbi Zvi Yehuda Kook, the evidence was plain. The prophetic predictions had already been transformed into a messianic reality. Recent events proved that the prophecies had come true.

"Thanks to God, the prophetic visions are unfolding before our very eyes," he wrote. "There is no more room for doubt or any question that might rattle our joy and our gratitude to the Redeemer of Israel."[4]

The comparison between God's messianic plan as revealed in Scripture and the course of Jewish history as it was unfolding in the State of Israel proved that the Redemption was coming. For the younger Rabbi Kook, the State of Israel did not herald the beginning of the Redemption: the State of Israel was already well into the advanced stages of the Redemption.[5] The younger Rabbi Kook, therefore, carved out for himself an appropriately historic role: to interpret the course of Zionist history as the story of the realization of God's messianic plans. "The real Redemption is already taking place in the advance of the settlement enterprise in the Land of Israel and in the resurrection of the state on that soil, in the continued renewal of settlement of the land thanks to the ingathering of the returning exiles, and in the restored control of our government over that land."[6]

Messianic Religious Zionists believe in a commandment to settle the Land of Israel and that this commandment differs from the other commandments in one key respect: its importance derives not from its significance in religious law but from its central role in the unfolding of a messianic drama. Settlements are the cause of Redemption, not merely a harbinger of it. For Rabbi Zvi Yehuda, the Redemption was not to be passively expected but actively expedited. The act that would bring about the Redemption was the settlement of the Land of Israel.[7]

No less important for Rabbi Zvi Yehuda, the commandment to settle the Land of Israel was also the main sphere in which the unwitting religiosity of secular Jews found its fullest expression.[8] Secular Israelis who built settlements and served in the army that protected those settlements were active participants in the fulfillment of the ancient prophecies and the forward march of history toward the era of final Redemption. Ironically, the secular Israelis who had no faith in the messianic agenda were the people bringing it to fruition. How could it be possible that the pioneers of the Redemption did not believe in the Redemption? Rabbi Zvi Yehuda theorized that their actions were evidence of their subconscious desire for it. Through their deeds they demonstrated their deep connection to the divine spirit of their people through a web of hidden, mystical threads.

THE THEOLOGICAL CRISIS OF THE DISENGAGEMENT

In the mind of Rabbi Kook the younger, the messianic process began with the First Aliyah (the first wave of immigration to Palestine, 1882–1903); accelerated with the establishment of the Jewish state; gained unstoppable momentum with the Six-Day War; advanced with the settlement of Judea, Samaria, and the Gaza Strip; and was destined to continue. The prophets had promised that the return from Exile was irreversible, as the prophet Amos declared: "And I will turn the captivity of My people Israel, and they shall build the waste cities, and inhabit them; and they shall plant vineyards, and drink the wine thereof; they shall also make gardens, and eat the fruit of them. And I will plant them upon their land, and they shall no more be plucked up out of their land which I have given them, sayeth the Lord thy God."[9]

The Redemption is a linear process, which advances and accelerates over time. As Rabbi Zvi Yehuda explained it, "God's historic decree to end the Exile, which is clear-cut and plainly visible, can be neither changed nor distorted. . . . The minor delays and postponements it might suffer could never conceivably put into reverse its forward march and its completely inevitable ascent."[10]

The messianic plan might run into minor delays, Rabbi Zvi Yehuda argued, but the messianic progress of Zionist history could never be reversed—a sense that was only heightened by the results of the Six-Day War. Thus responded Rabbi Yaakov Filber, a student of Kook the younger, to calls to relinquish some of the land conquered by the IDF during the war: "I believe with complete faith that if the Holy One Blessed Be He openly delivered us this land, He will never wrest it from our hands. *The Lord does not perform miracles in vain.*"[11]

Let us look carefully at what Rabbi Filber both did and did not say. He did not say that it was *forbidden* to relinquish the territories liberated in the war; he determined that they categorically *would not be* relinquished. The settler leader Hanan Porat expressed a similar position on the eve of the evacuation of the Sinai Peninsula. He explained that a withdrawal from any part of the Land of Israel was simply metaphysically impossible—and to believe it might actually happen was nothing but superstition.[12] "We have to teach ourselves," he said, "that the notion of a withdrawal is every bit as fantastical as ghosts."[13]

Rabbi Zvi Yehuda Kook died a few weeks before the final evacuation of the Jewish settlements in the Sinai Desert. Some might have predicted that the demolition of these settlements would cause his followers to abandon Kook's philosophy, and that the withdrawal would provoke the collapse of the messianic stream of Religious Zionism. But that is not what happened. There was certainly a crisis, but the messianic school of history survived the first event that was supposed to discredit it. Then came another, more powerful crisis: twenty-three years after the evacuation of the Sinai Peninsula, Israel decided to uproot the community of Gush Katif in the Gaza Strip.

Israel was rocked by a major wave of protests as the Disengagement Plan—the evacuation of settlers from the entire Gaza Strip and parts of northern Samaria—approached implementation in 2005. The disciples of Rabbi Zvi Yehuda already had thousands of followers of their own. Many of the families who lived in Gush Katif refused to prepare for the approaching day of evacuation, neither packing their belongings nor making arrangements for where to go. They continued to behave as though the eviction would never occur. Porat's prediction on the eve of the evacuation of the Sinai Peninsula became the widespread assumption on the eve of the evacuation of the Gaza Strip: "It just won't happen."[14]

But this forecast was again proven wrong, and the crisis of faith that should have erupted after the Sinai evacuation struck after the evacuation of Gush Katif and northern Samaria instead.

After the Disengagement, Rabbi Moshe Tzuriel described the prospect that Rabbi Kook might have been mistaken as a possibility that had to be confronted: "Is *this* really the 'beginning of the growth of our redemption'? If Rabbi Abraham Isaac Kook were alive in this generation, do you think he would still declare that we are deep into the Redemption? Or would he swallow his words instead? Perhaps it would be wiser and more responsible of us to draw the conclusion that Rabbi Kook was simply wrong."[15]

When the State of Israel evicted the settlers from the entire Gaza Strip and parts of northern Samaria, it did not just demolish the settlements themselves—it demolished the messianic idea that had encouraged the settlers to build those settlements in the first place. The uprooting of settlements was to Religious Zionism what the privatization of the kibbutzim was to socialist Zionism: an ideological blow from which it would struggle to recover.

Not everyone despaired. Efforts to continue justifying the messianic interpretation of Zionism continued well after the Disengagement.[16] Rabbi Zvi Tau of the messianic Merkaz HaRav Yeshiva proposed that stepping back from parts of the Land of Israel was not a step back from the Redemption but an integral part thereof. "The stages of withdrawal and crisis are also part of our journey of ascent," he argued. "They constitute training and preparation for the next stage of the Salvation."[17]

But if messianic faith in Zionism could still be justified, it was much harder to justify messianic faith in secular society. The Disengagement had proven that the secular State of Israel would not only plant settlements but uproot them; the secular Israeli army would not only protect settlements but also demolish them. The theory that secular Israelis were the unknowing pioneers of the Redemption fell apart when it became clear that they were the fully conscious pioneers of the retreat from Redemption. As a result, the religious justification for cooperation with secular Zionists suffered a mortal blow.[18]

This feeling was most clearly expressed by Rabbi Zalman Melamed, another disciple of Rabbi Zvi Yehuda: "Perhaps the Religious Zionist movement was wrong to think it could forge ties with secular Zionism. . . . Perhaps the whole dream of co-existence and of ever finding a way to bring the faithless closer to faith was a pipe dream. *Perhaps those who argued that there was no point in becoming close to secular folk because their way is the opposite of ours were right after all* (emphasis mine)."[19]

The blow that the Disengagement struck the messianic understanding of Zionism pales in comparison, therefore, with the blow it struck the mystical interpretation of secularism. Rabbi Kook the elder wrote that the secular Jews' sense of peoplehood was bound to draw them back to religion. But in reality, the opposite occurred. Nationalism did not transform secularism: secularism transformed nationalism instead. Secularism provoked a form of nationalism among Religious Zionists that found justification not only in the Bible but in the soil and in dreams of redemption as well.[20]

In the philosophy of Jabotinsky, as we saw, serious tension existed between liberalism and territorial maximalism. In the philosophy of Rabbi Zvi Yehuda Kook, an equally serious tension exists between a firm devotion to the Torah and a mystical connection to a nation that does not obey the Torah. And just as Jabotinsky's philosophy disintegrated into its constituent parts over time, Religious Zionism is now at risk of disintegrating into its constituent parts. The idea that was supposedly vindicated by one historic event—the Six-Day War—was fatally weakened by another historic event—the Disengagement.

MESSIANIC RELIGIOUS ZIONISM AND THE ISRAELI CRISIS OF POLITICAL IDEAS

The waning of the right-wing messianic movement, however, did not diminish the right overall. On the contrary, the Disengagement ended up strengthening it. Consider how. The religious right based its agenda on two foundations—security and Redemption. Since the summer of 2005, the messianic argument has been weakened, but the security argument has been fortified. The same Disengagement that shook the right's conviction about Redemption also amplified its concerns about security.

Before the Disengagement, pessimists prophesied that a unilateral withdrawal would endanger Israel's security. They argued that any territory vacated by the IDF would be seized by the forces of radical Islamism to launch missiles into Israeli cities. These prophecies of doom came true within a short time. The same Disengagement that undermined the right's arguments about mysticism, therefore, also bolstered its arguments about security. This was the birth of the latest incarnation of the Israeli right—a right anchored predominantly in the promise of security, rather than the hope of the Redemption.

In response, the left underwent its own process of reincarnation.[21] Just as the right matured and moved on from talking about the Redemption, the left matured and moved on from talking about peace. The left replaced its hopes for peace with concerns about the crimes of occupation. Mainstream left-wing discourse today focuses not so much on the virtues of peace as on the human rights violations inherent in continued military rule.

The new right and the new left are mirror images. The new left no longer argues that withdrawing from the territories will bring peace. Rather, leftists maintain that sustaining a military presence there will bring disaster. The new right no longer argues that settling the territories will bring redemption. Right-wingers claim that withdrawing from them will bring disaster. Both have replaced their greatest hopes with their darkest fears.

I have illustrated, in brief, the history of two compelling ideas: the story of how both the left and right metamorphosed twice. Those on the right began life as liberals, developed into messianists, and now limp along thinking mostly about security. Those on the left arose as socialists, then dreamt of peace, and now focus mostly on human rights and the evils of occupation. This is the story of how Israel was delivered from the past certainties of its robust ideologies to its present reality of utter confusion.

PART II POLITICAL IDEAS IN CRISIS

And if we persevere in fighting for what is close to our hearts, we must avoid becoming fixated on our feelings and know that the world is wide enough to contain feelings contrary to our own.

—Rabbi Abraham Isaac Kook

INTRODUCTION

Both Sides Are Right

Whereas in the previous section I focused on the history of Israel's political ideologies, in this one I shall deal with the logic of Israel's assorted political arguments. Despite the interrelatedness between ideologies and arguments, there is a crucial difference. Ideologies are clusters of ideas that provide their adherents with an identity. Revisionism, socialism, messianism, and peace have become organic parts of the identity of many Israelis. Arguments, however, do not cultivate identities; they justify courses of action. Arguments do not produce intellectual worldviews; they justify practical policies.

Israel's political arguments have fallen into crisis, just as its ideologies have. But this is a different kind of crisis. Israel's ideological crises occurred when those ideologies failed to comport with reality. Israel's political arguments, however, remain cogent. Reality has not discredited them—it has vindicated them. Over time, almost all the political arguments voiced in Israel today have emerged as correct. The right wing is correct, and so is the left wing. The arguments for both sides have proven valid. Hence the crisis.

I shall turn my attention now to elucidating and analyzing these arguments. I shall look at the right's argument about the imperatives of security and the left's argument about the inevitabilities of demography. This will enable us to confront the difficult ethical problems about the occupation raised by the left, while keeping in mind the right's historical position that there is no "occupation" at all. I shall then consider the argument that a retreat from Judea and Samaria would be a retreat from Jewish identity, while also considering whether military rule over a civilian population violates the vision of the Jewish prophets.

Finally, I shall focus on how retaining the territories offends the vision of Zionism on the one hand while realizing the Zionist dream on the other. This section of the book offers a journey into the depths of the internal logic of four arguments: existential, ethical, Jewish, and Zionist. Together, they form the basis of the new reality of the deep and comprehensive confusion that is engulfing Israeli politics today.

4 A CONFUSING PARADOX

THE INHERENT DIFFICULTIES OF ISRAEL'S POSITION

Israel's existence is threatened by its location. Israel is a liberal democracy surrounded by anti-Western cultural forces that view its presence in the Middle East as a Western invasion of Arab territory. Israel is also a Jewish state surrounded by anti-Semitic forces that view any non-Muslim sovereignty in the realm of Islam as an offense against God. These two mighty forces—the one desiring to expel the Western invasion, and the other desiring to cleanse the realm of Islam—have merged to form a powerful axis of resistance against Israel's existence.[1]

Israel is threatened not only because of its position, but also because of its area. Israel is so narrow that the IDF has no room for maneuvering to prepare effectively to repel enemy advances. These intrinsic difficulties threaten the State of Israel's survival. Because of its location and its area, Israel is encircled by enemies and is challenged to defend itself against them.[2]

These difficult conditions heighten the importance of the mountains of Judea and Samaria to Israel's security. Owing to

Israel's population distribution and geographic features, the country simply cannot be defended without this territory. Demographically, the narrow coastal plain is home to the vast majority of Israel's Jewish population. Seventy percent of Israel's citizens reside on this plain, and 80 percent of its industrial capacity is concentrated there.[3] This area is the cultural capital and economic heart of the State of Israel, with the most densely packed Jewish population in the world.

Geographically, the coastal plain is located by the foothills of the mountains of Judea and Samaria, which loom over it from the east. The mountain range rises to an elevation of over 1,000 meters (3,200 feet) above sea level before descending sharply into the depths of the Jordan Valley. These mountains and this valley are the only geographic buffer between a vast Arab world and a tightly packed Jewish population. The conclusion is straightforward: whoever controls the mountains controls the nerve center of the entire Jewish people.

The question that remains to be answered is, Who controls this mountain range? The ridge could serve as the base for a devastating attack on the largest concentration of Jews in the world, but it could also serve as an effective buffer for their defense. When the IDF is entrenched atop these mountains, not only is it impossible for the Arabs to use them to attack the center of Israel, it is much easier to defend that center. By controlling the mountain range Israel maintains a topographical buffer zone between the Tel Aviv metropolitan area and the vast Muslim-Arab world beyond.

Conversely, were Israel to retreat from these mountains, this would create a power vacuum that would be filled by the chaos engulfing the Middle East, bringing it to the very doorstep of Tel Aviv. A withdrawal would create unbroken Arab-held territory stretching from Baghdad to Netanya. It would transform Israel's core into borderlands abutting a perilous frontier. The mountains of Judea and Samaria form a defensive barrier that divides the unstable Arab world from the relatively stable Western world in Israel. Without this territory, no one could promise Israel that its world would remain either Western or peaceful.

THE DEMOGRAPHIC PROBLEM

As a rule, the population growth rates of developed countries differ from those of developing countries. The difference between the Israeli and Palestinian population growth rates presents what Israelis call the demographic problem: Since the Palestinian population is increasing at a faster pace than that of the Jews, the Palestinian population is certain, over time, to surpass the Jewish population in numbers. The Jewish relative majority is contracting, and the day is fast approaching when most of the inhabitants of Israel will no longer be Jewish. In this forecast, which some demographers dispute, the Jewish state is in danger.[4] The demographic trend threatens Israel's continued existence as the nation-state of the Jewish people. The day the Jews become a minority in their own land will be the day they cease being the masters of their own fate.

The Jewish population of Israel is a small minority in the Middle East, but it is still a clear majority within the borders of pre-1967 Israel. Throughout its history, Israel has successfully resisted attacks by the Muslim majority around it. Looking to the future, however, the Jews have no chance of holding their ground in the face of a Muslim majority inside the state. The end of Zionism will not come through conquest from without but through demographic changes within.

"I have performed a cold calculation," noted the Israeli demographer Arnon Soffer of the University of Haifa. "We are facing the end of the State of Israel."[5]

In this alarming scenario, Zionism will not meet its end because the Jews will return to being minorities in the nation-states from which they came but because they will become a minority in the nation-state they inhabit now. But the end of Zionism is not the only possible result of this demographic scenario. There exists another: that Israel's Jewish minority will continue to rule the country despite being a minority and will do so by force of arms. The State of Israel would continue to be Jewish in such a scenario, but it would no longer be democratic.

This is the beating heart of the demographic problem. The day is fast approaching when Israel will face an impossible dilemma— to be ruled as a minority by a non-Jewish majority, or to rule over that non-Jewish majority by force. Israelis will have to decide whether they want Israel to be Jewish but no longer democratic or democratic but no longer Jewish. Whatever happens, it would mean the end of the State of Israel as they now know it.

Israel's War of Independence turned decisively in July 1948 when the IDF began to gain ground against the Arab armies. The invading forces began to retreat, and the IDF started to enlarge the areas under its control. From a military perspective, the IDF could have conquered the entire West Bank at that point. Indeed, the IDF top brass raised such a possibility with Prime Minister David Ben-Gurion.[6] They advised him to take advantage of the army's momentum and seize the opportunity to capture Judea and Samaria, turning the Jordan River into the eastern border of the new state. But Ben-Gurion shot down the proposal: "The IDF can capture the entire territory between the river and the sea. But what sort of country would that give us? . . . We would have a Knesset with an Arab majority. Faced with either a Greater Israel or a Jewish Israel, we choose a Jewish Israel."[7]

Ben-Gurion, gifted with a profound appreciation of history and Scripture, understood that the conquest of Judea and Samaria would bequeath to Israel far more than the land. This small area is the repository of the foundational memories of the Jewish people. Without Judea and Samaria, the Land of Israel would be incomplete. The problem was that this territory contained not only memories but people. If it were made part of a democratic State of Israel, its inhabitants would also belong to that state. Ironically, the annexation of territory containing such ancient Jewish resonance would have abolished modern Jewish sovereignty. Confronted with the dilemma of having either a Jewish minority over the whole of the land or a Jewish majority over part of the land, Ben-Gurion opted decisively for a Jewish majority —and therefore against capturing Judea and Samaria.

But that which failed to happen during the War of Independence occurred later in the Six-Day War. Israel's swift and mighty victory ended with the conquest in 1967 of the territories it had chosen not to conquer in 1948. Ben-Gurion's dilemma returned with a vengeance, this time in reverse. In 1948, Ben-Gurion debated whether to conquer the territory; since 1967, Israelis have been debating whether to withdraw from it. The question has been turned on its head, but the crux remains the same:

Should Israel prefer a Jewish minority over the whole of the land or a Jewish majority over part of it?

Ben-Gurion's decision to forgo the conquest of these territories rescued the ideal of Jewish sovereignty at the birth of the state, and it would seem that repeating this decision—through a withdrawal from the territories—would save the ideal of Jewish sovereignty today.

Although some demographers continue to dispute the factual basis of the demographic problem, as I shall discuss below, most agree that the Jewish majority west of the Jordan River is living on borrowed time. The author Amos Oz summarized the situation succinctly: "If there will not be two states here, and fast, there will be one state here. If there will be one state here, it will be an Arab state, from the sea to the Jordan River."[8]

Let me recap the two central arguments: From a security perspective, Israel must not withdraw from the territories; but from a demographic perspective, Israel must not remain there. If Israel withdraws, its area shrinks to indefensible proportions, but if it remains, its Jewish majority is in danger. The two contrary positions create a confusing paradox: Israel must never withdraw from these territories, yet at the same time Israel must withdraw from these territories.

5 NO SECURITY PROBLEM?

Some on the Israeli left deny the existence of the paradox governing the perils of remaining in the territories and of relinquishing them. They maintain that although the demographic problem remains severe and acute, the security threat has been fabricated. If withdrawal brings peace, after all, then that withdrawal will not undermine Israel's security; it will buttress it. A peace accord would presumably include security arrangements with guarantees from the international community, and would redeem Israel from its present international isolation. Any treaty with the Palestinians would have to be endorsed by the Arab League and the world community, and it would thus completely transform Israel's international standing. Israel would cease to be an isolated fortress-state constantly on the defensive against its own neighbors and instead become a country integrated into and at peace with those around it. The fruits of a peace accord, the left concludes, would make Israel stronger and more resilient than it is today.

The left's security argument can be rephrased thus: The territories are a security asset, but so is a peace treaty—and the diplomatic resource of a peace treaty is of greater security value than the territorial resource of Judea and Samaria. To exchange the territories for a lasting peace, therefore, is not to weaken Israel's security but to strengthen it. A withdrawal might make the country more difficult to defend in wartime, but a peace treaty would end the present state of war altogether.

This argument is based on two mistaken assumptions. The first assumption unjustly minimizes the power of this historic conflict; the second unjustly maximizes the power of any possible diplomatic accord. Let us turn our attention now to these two fallacies.

THE RATIONALE OF RESISTANCE: THE *MUQAWAMA*

The hatred that Palestinians feel toward Israelis is rooted partly in the broader hatred of the Arab and Islamic worlds toward what they perceive as continued Western imperialism. The rise of the West and the decline of Islam have seared a sense of humiliation into the Muslim mind.[1] National resistance to Western imperialism, *muqawama* in Arabic, constitutes a refusal to accept the disparity in power between the two civilizations—and therefore a refusal to accept the physical presence and cultural influence of anything Western on Muslim lands.[2] Muqawama is a struggle whose value is independent of its results: merely to persevere is to refuse to surrender to foreign humiliation.[3] It is a struggle whose importance is in its existence—a struggle for the sake of struggle. Under this reasoning, a peace treaty that would end all the Palestinians' claims and terminate their national struggle would be nothing but an act of surrender to Western supremacy and an acceptance of Islamic inferiority. Making peace with Israel would be perceived by many Muslims as making peace with the West's encroachment onto Muslim lands.

To free the Israeli-Arab conflict from the historical weight of this perceived Islamic-Western rivalry, the Palestinians would have to divorce their national consciousness from their historic Islamic consciousness. If they succeeded, they would stop seeing the conflict as an outgrowth of the clash between the Islamic and Western worlds, and would see it instead as a clash between Israelis and Palestinians alone. If the Palestinians could reframe their national identity, the conflict need no longer be tied to the decline and humiliation of Islam.

But even in this hypothetical scenario, the historical weight of the conflict would remain too heavy. Even if the Palestinians recognized that a conflict between nations is not a clash of civilizations, its historical weight would frustrate attempts to achieve a diplomatic solution. For at the heart of the Palestinians' historical memory is not the occupation of 1967 but the expulsion of 1948.

THE NAKBA

The War of Independence produced the State of Israel, but it also produced the specter that has haunted Israel's existence ever since: the Palestinian refugee problem. The war provoked a massive exodus.[4] Hundreds of thousands of Arabs left what became the State of Israel for neighboring Arab countries. Of the 950,000 Arabs who lived in what is now the State of Israel on the eve of the 1948 war, some 700,000 either fled or were expelled during the course of hostilities.[5] When the guns fell silent, the

Arab refugees were confronted with the unambiguous policy of the Israeli government to forbid them to return home. This war, which left some 80 percent of the Palestinians uprooted from their homes, fragmented Palestinian society and scattered its members to the four winds.

Today the descendants of these refugees number between five and seven million people, many of whom still reside in refugee camps dispersed across Jordan, Syria, Lebanon, the West Bank, and the Gaza Strip. The camps are administered by the United Nations Relief and Works Agency (UNRWA), an organization established to deal exclusively with Palestinian refugees.[6] Of all the waves of mass population movement in the mid-twentieth century, the Palestinian situation is the only case in which the descendants of the original refugees are automatically defined as refugees themselves.[7]

Researchers who have visited the refugee camps, where so many of the refugees still live, report that the inhabitants retain memories of the homes from which they were expelled, as well as hope that they will one day return to those homes. When the older children in one refugee camp in Lebanon were asked to draw their homes, they drew not the dwellings in which they actually lived but houses located in Haifa or Safed.[8] The entrances of many of these camps feature sculptures of keys, representing the keys of houses in Israel of which the residents were dispossessed. Many Palestinian cartoons include the figure of a child wearing the key to the family's former house in Jaffa or Haifa around his or her neck.

The event that shattered Palestinian society, then, also forged the Palestinian national memory. Known simply as "the Catastrophe," the Nakba has been seared into the Palestinians' collective consciousness and has become an integral part of their identity. Those who hold this identity see themselves on a timeline with a distinct past and a clear future. The past is the expulsion; the future, return. Most Palestinians believe that all the refugees have a right to return to the homes from which they were expelled: they call this *haqq al-ʿawda*, "right of return." They also expect that this right will be recognized one day, and that the refugees will be able to return to their national land and to their private lands. Since the right of return is central to the Palestinians' identity, they cannot forgo it without changing the essence of that national identity.[9]

The full realization of this Palestinian national aspiration would spell the end of Zionism. If hundreds of thousands of refugees returned to their former homes, the national home of the Jewish people would cease to exist.[10] This is why the solution of two states for two peoples would require the Palestinians to forgo the return of masses of Palestinians into the sovereign territory of the State of Israel. In a two-state solution, Israel would transfer the territories it conquered in 1967 to Palestinian sovereignty, and in return the Palestinians would cede their professed right to return to the lands they held before the 1948 war. This is the deal on the table: Israel will make peace by leaving the territory captured in 1967, and the Palestinians will make peace by ceding the land beyond the 1948 lines.

Could the Palestinians possibly accept such a deal? And if they could, would such a deal be sustainable? If earlier we saw that a peace treaty would require the Palestinians to detach their historic memory from their broader Islamic sense of humiliation, it now seems that they would have to detach their historic memory from their own national sense of humiliation.

Rarely do Israelis understand that their demand that the Palestinians cede the right of return is effectively a demand for the Palestinians to deny their own identity. Moreover, Israel's expectation that the Palestinians would come to terms with the events of 1948 in exchange for a reversal of the events of 1967 is the expectation that the Palestinians would betray their own nation.[11] Such a deal would be perceived as treason against the hundreds of thousands of Palestinians still living in dozens of refugee camps.[12] Israelis refuse to acknowledge any of this history when they stubbornly insist that the heart of the conflict is the occupation of 1967.

To summarize, the Israeli-Palestinian conflict has three components: the centuries-long trauma of Islam's humiliation by the West; the decades-long trauma of the mass Palestinian exodus during the War of Independence; and the fifty-year trauma of occupation and military rule from the Six-Day War to the present.[13] The solution of two states for two peoples addresses only the third component.

No treaty that terminated the military occupation but failed to solve the refugee problem could hope to end the conflict. A treaty that removed the IDF from territories captured in the Six-Day War but left the Islamic world feeling inferior in the face of Western superiority would not address the Palestinians' basic identity needs. Diplomatic solutions proposed thus far for ending this conflict are flimsy and paper-thin—but the problem remains deep and inflexible. The asymmetry between problem and proposed solutions is itself a fundamental problem.

Israel does not have the power to erase the centuries of Islamic humiliation by the West that nourish the Palestinians' national struggle against Zionism. Israel does not have the power to erase the trauma of the Nakba without surrendering its own identity and existence. The Arab-Israeli conflict was not created by the IDF's conquest of the territories in the Six-Day War. Historically, the opposite is true: the conflict provoked the IDF's conquest of the territories in the first place.

The occupation, then, is but one of the many roots of this intractable conflict. Crucially, however, the occupation is the only root over which Israel has any power. This, I believe, is the psychological reason why many Israelis find it so tempting to imagine that the occupation is the core of the problem. The belief that the occupation is the historic heart of this conflict gives Israelis a sense of control over history. Conversely, the recognition that the roots of the conflict are out of their hands is something Israelis find too painful to accept. Westerners tend to struggle to internalize the notion that history might be bigger than they are, and that not everything is under their control.

If the situation is as I have described it, no diplomatic accord could end the violent conflict between Israel and the Palestinians —just as no diplomatic accord could compensate Israel for the inherent danger to its security posed by a withdrawal from the mountains of Judea and Samaria.

6 NO DEMOGRAPHIC PROBLEM?

The conclusion arrived at in the previous chapter was simple and straightforward: Israel must not withdraw from the territories it captured in the Six-Day War. The problem, however, is that Israel cannot afford to remain in them either. Israel's continued presence in the territories threatens to isolate the country diplomatically and endanger it demographically. Israel's diplomatic isolation, at least with respect to Europe, is only deepening, just as its demographic situation is deteriorating. Every additional year that Israel fails to vacate the territories is a year its Jewish majority becomes more fragile and its international isolation more painful.

These two trends are connected: when the demographic judgment day arrives, international patience will finally snap. When the Jewish minority finds itself ruling an Arab majority by force of arms, Israel will not only cease to be a democracy; it will cease to be a member of the family of nations.

Some on the Israeli right acknowledge both the diplomatic threat and the problem of sustaining rule over a noncitizen population. Their political solution is the annexation of the West Bank to the State of Israel. In such a scenario, the inhabitants of the territories would not be subjects ruled over by the State of Israel—they would become its citizens. This simple policy, the right believes, would save Israel from the twin dangers of diplomatic isolation and democratic erosion.

Yet would not such a process undercut Israel's self-definition as the nation-state of the Jewish people? We have already seen that if the left's political solution, the two-state solution, endangers Israel's ability to defend itself, then the political solution of the right, the creation of a single state between the Jordan River and the Mediterranean Sea, endangers Israel's ability to define itself. The advocates of annexation reject this equation outright. They maintain that Israel can annex Judea and Samaria together with their inhabitants while remaining both Jewish and democratic because they dispute the existence of the demographic danger. They argue that the so-called demographic problem does not exist—it is a fiction invented by left-wing Israeli demographers based not on hard facts but on fictitious and inflated statistics borrowed from the Palestinian Authority.[1]

In the estimation of these dissenting demographers, the territories contain hundreds of thousands fewer Arabs than the conventional demographers calculate. And not only are there fewer Arabs than commonly thought: their population is also growing much more slowly than it did in the past. These right-wing demographers maintain that there has been a dramatic shift in both Palestinian and Israeli birthrates within the past two decades: the Palestinian birthrate is dropping, while the Israeli birthrate continues to rise. As a result, eventually the Arabs will no longer reproduce at a faster rate than the Jews—and this, the right-wing demographers conclude, means the demographic problem does not exist.

From here, it is only a short hop to the conclusion that since the Jewish majority west of the Jordan River is under no danger of becoming a minority, Israel can safely annex all the residents of Judea and Samaria without threatening the Jewish character of the country.[2]

There are two logical fallacies inherent in the denial of the demographic problem. The first speaks to the internal contradiction in the right's attitudes toward the population estimates; the second derives from the right's irrational approach to risk calculation. Let us examine both these fallacies.

THE FALLACY OF THE RIGHT'S ATTITUDES TOWARD THE PALESTINIAN POPULATION ESTIMATES

The right-wing objection to claims of a demographic problem is based on the conclusions of an American demographic study whose chief proponent in Israel is Yoram Ettinger, a former diplomat and a member of the American-Israel Demographic Research Group (AIDRG). This is the dispute in brief: According to Arnon Soffer, the expert speaking for the Israeli academic establishment, there were 2.54 million Arabs in Judea and Samaria as of 2016.[3] Ettinger disputes this calculation and claims that there were only 1.75 million Arabs in Judea and Samaria that year.[4] The discrepancy between these two estimates is therefore a difference of nearly one million people. The right argues that the left, because of its clear interests, inflates the numbers; the left argues that the right, because of *its* clear interests, understates them. I cannot claim to arbitrate between demographers, but for the sake of argument, let us side with Ettinger for a moment. Given this lower figure, could Israel still annex such a sizable Arab population without destabilizing itself?

The reason that the annexation of so many Palestinians would undermine Israel's self-definition as the nation-state of the Jewish people is that that definition depends on retaining not only a Jewish majority but a clear and decisive Jewish majority. The annexation of 1.75 million Palestinians to the State of Israel, which already contains around 1.7 million Arab citizens, would double Israel's non-Jewish population. Israel's Arab population would become a very large minority indeed, and it would demand a role appropriate for its size in the governance of the country. This dramatic jump in the size of the Arab population in Israel would bring it within just a few years to 40 percent of the country's total population. That figure is based only on the present size of both populations, without considering the major disparities between the different forecasts of natural growth.[5]

Such a number would already constitute a critical mass, with tremendous cultural and political weight. Is it difficult to imagine, for example, an alliance between a large, anti-Zionist Muslim minority and a small, post-Zionist Jewish minority to abolish Israel's Law of Return or replace the national anthem? If such a thing seems possible, then even if the demographers on the right are correct that the Jews would still be a majority after an annexation, they would no longer be a decisive majority—and the State of Israel would struggle to define itself as the nation-state of the Jewish people. It would be the state of two nations residing within it. Even if we can accept Ettinger's calculations, we cannot accept the conclusions that purportedly follow.

Those on the right who campaign for a single sovereign state west of the Jordan River believe that the State of Israel is strong enough to withstand a very large Palestinian minority inside it. This is the mirror image of the left's argument, that the State of Israel is strong enough to defend itself from a Palestinian state located right next to it. But the expansion of the state's borders would come at the price of the contraction of the state's Jewish majority—a contraction so dramatic that it would undercut Israel's self-definition as the nation-state of the Jewish people.[6]

Note the following intellectual shortcoming in the position that rejects a Palestinian state but simultaneously supports the annexation of the Palestinians. Generally, Israelis' objections to the establishment of a Palestinian state next to Israel derive from their lack of faith in the peaceful intentions of the Palestinian people. This raises the question, How can someone who has no faith in the Palestinians as citizens of a future Palestinian state have faith in the same people as citizens of the Israeli state? If they cannot be trusted as partners at the negotiating table, how can they be trusted as partners at the Cabinet table? This problem should bedevil the advocates of annexation on the right: if the Palestinians are undeserving of the confidence of the State of Israel, why should they be given citizenship en masse in that same state?[7]

THE FALLACY OF THE RIGHT'S IRRATIONAL RISK CALCULATION

There is disagreement over the number of Palestinians in the territories today, and there is disagreement over their numbers in the future. There is no disagreement about the fact that there is disagreement. And there is no disagreement that demography is far from an exact science and that future projections are subject to factors that cannot be predicted, such as changes in immigration patterns or shifts in fertility rates or in life expectancy. Demographers must treat with caution their own ability to predict the future, explains the researcher Robi Nathanson, because even tiny political, economic, health care, and cultural changes can generate major demographic changes over time. And since nobody can predict the aggregate of these tiny changes, nobody can confidently predict major demographic changes well into the future.[8]

The Israeli right demands that people exercise caution when making predictions concerning the end of Israel's Jewish majority, and it is correct to do so—but by the same measure, the right itself must exercise caution when predicting that demographics pose no danger. Even those convinced that Ettinger's minority opinion is the more reasonable demographic estimate must recognize that he might be wrong. Even if it is more likely that the demographic problem does not exist, it is still possible that the demographic problem might exist. Any right-wingers with a shred of intellectual honesty must take into account the risk that the left's demographic nightmare could yet come true.

In a rational calculation of that risk, given the demographic assumptions of the right, the loss of Israel's Jewish majority is an unlikely but still devastating prospect—a high-impact, low-probability event. Betting on a one-state solution is like investing in a stock that analysts say has a small chance of falling but would be totally wiped out if it fell. No rational or responsible investors would put all their money in such a stock. This is the crux of the irrationality of right-wing supporters of annexation: they are willing to bet 100 percent of Israel's survival on this one demographic stock. Nobody would board a plane who suspected there might be even a 10 percent chance that the plane would crash simply because the likelihood was low.

I shall recap my criticism in brief. It is possible to predict that the Jewish majority will not be wiped out in the foreseeable future; my criticism is not of the right's demographic forecasts but of the leap from making such predictions to making policy. It is neither reasonable nor rational to attempt to derive a policy of settlement expansion or annexation based on Ettinger's forecasts, for both the reasons I have discussed. First, even without neutralizing the Jewish majority, an annexation of the territories would shrink that majority and thereby undermine Israel's self-definition as the nation-state of the Jewish people. Second, total reliance on the optimistic demographic scenario represents a risk calculation so irrational as to constitute an unreasonable gamble that endangers the continuity and survival of the Zionist project.

IS THERE APARTHEID IN THE TERRITORIES?

Judea and Samaria are under Israeli military rule, but the Palestinian inhabitants there are not Israeli citizens. This fact casts serious doubt on the democratic character of the State of Israel. The Jewish-American journalist Peter Beinart phrased it thus: the State of Israel is divided in two, a democratic Israel that reaches the Green Line (the pre-1967 boundary) and a nondemocratic Israel that exists beyond the Green Line.[9]

The settlement enterprise exacerbates this problem because

it creates a situation in which citizens of Israel and subjects of Israel inhabit the same land.[10] The distinctions between these two classes of residents make it difficult for Israel to reject the comparison of the situation in the territories to South Africa's former system of apartheid. Is this comparison accurate? Is Israel not a democracy after all? Has it instituted apartheid in the territories?

The situation is extremely complicated and must be examined with sensitivity. Under Israeli law, the current legal status of the territories is considered temporary. Israel's position is that the primary reason why no Palestinian state has yet emerged is that the Palestinian leadership has for years been refusing to accept one in negotiations. The situation is confusing because it is paradoxical: the status quo is perpetuated not at the insistence of the occupiers but by the rejectionism of the occupied.

There would appear to be a problem to this argument—specifically, that there *is* another way to end Israel's rule over people who are not its citizens: give them citizenship. But herein lies the main reason why the comparison between Israel and the apartheid regime of South Africa breaks down. The struggle of the Palestinian national movement is fundamentally different from that of the African National Congress. Whereas the blacks in South Africa demanded to be made equal citizens of their country, the Palestinian national movement is not demanding to be *part of* the State of Israel—it is demanding the creation of an independent state *apart from* Israel.

Why do the Palestinians not follow the example of the blacks of South Africa and demand Israeli citizenship? If they revised the aim of their struggle, and converted it from one for independence *from* Israel into one for citizenship *of* Israel, they would put Israel on the spot. Why do they not do this? They do not because such a demand would be taken as tacit recognition of the State of Israel in its current form. To express the desire to be citizens of the Jewish state would be akin to expressing the desire to collaborate with the Zionist project, or at least to accepting the legitimacy of the national aspirations of the Jewish people. In this sense, a demand for Israeli citizenship would be perceived by most Palestinians as an act of national betrayal. One could argue that the Palestinians' failure to demand Israeli citizenship is one of the primary reasons why Israel is not an apartheid state.

But the day the Palestinians become the majority population, a collective demand for Israeli citizenship would no longer be perceived as support for the Jewish state—it would clearly be seen as a demand for the elimination of the Jewish state as such. Given this, if the demographic judgment day arrives, the Palestinians will probably convert the nature of their struggle. Instead of demanding that a state be established on a portion of the land, they will demand the right to vote for members of the Knesset —and thereby to become the ruling majority over the whole of the land. The transformation of the population statistics will cause the transformation of the national struggle, and that in turn will cause the transformation of the State of Israel. When demographic conditions enable the Palestinians to campaign for the same objective as the blacks of South Africa, Israel could become South Africa.

The inescapable conclusion is that only as long as the Jews remain a majority in their land can they still divide that land. This is why the demographic problem is so pressing for those on the right who do not support annexation. The perpetuation of the status quo is possible only as long as the Palestinian struggle is for independence, but this situation is temporary. It is not clear how long Israel has until the demographic window of opportunity finally closes—but it was a wise person who said, "The Palestinian state is the Jewish state's lifeline."[11]

THE FALLACY ON THE LEFT AND THE IDEOLOGICAL DOUBLE BIND

The same criticism of irrational risk calculation levied against the pro-annexation right, however, must also be applied to the pro-withdrawal left. The dominant argument on the left is that the security arrangements that would underpin a peace treaty would provide Israel with security even without the occupation of Judea and Samaria. International forces, for example, could be stationed in the Jordan Valley to guarantee both Palestine's demilitarization and Israel's peace of mind.

But what if this argument were also mistaken? The left must accept its own element of risk and the certain possibility that it too might be wrong. Even if the risk is assessed to be low, the risky scenario remains catastrophic. Just as the right is gambling on a national majority, the left is gambling on national security.

Consider how a rational conversation about the conflict might go. Everyone would agree that the security risk identified by the right had a certain weight and that the demographic risk identified by the left also had weight—the debate would be over *how much* weight to assign each risk. But as it stands, the right argues that the demographic risk involved in remaining in Judea and Samaria can be contained and managed, while the risk involved in withdrawing is insurmountable. The left, for its part, maintains that the risk involved in withdrawing can be contained, while the risk involved in not withdrawing is greater tenfold.

If this conversation were rational rather than ideological, the sides would recognize both dangers but disagree on how much importance to attach to them. Israeli political discourse, however, does not work this way. Instead, each side highlights *one* danger while totally denying the other.

The right's denial of the demographic risk is deeply rooted, as is the left's denial of the territorial security risk. The left's primary identification tends to be with the West. Left-wing Israelis mostly identify with Western culture, and favor a cosmopolitan and universalistic outlook. The right's primary identification, meanwhile, tends to be more Jewish and nationalistic. Its outlook is predominantly traditional and religious.

One of the lessons of Western history, as witnessed and taught in the late twentieth and early twenty-first centuries, is that every attempt by a Western power to conquer land and rule over another people has ended in failure. This is a lesson that Israelis must learn, and they must stop ruling over another people.

But Jewish history has a profound lesson to teach as well. The lesson learned from centuries of Jewish history is that when the fate and security of the Jews are left in foreign hands, the result is disaster. The lesson learned from Jewish history is that the security of the Jews must never be entrusted to non-Jews. As David Ben-Gurion said, "Even in places where the Jews appeared secure, they always lacked a sense of security. Why? Because even when they were safe, it was not they who were responsible for their own safety."[12] The conclusion to be drawn from

Jewish history is that Israelis must not deposit the security of the residents of Israel's coastal plain in the hands of the residents of the mountains by withdrawing from Judea and Samaria—and certainly not out of faith in international guarantees.

Before us is a clash between the lessons of Western history and the lessons of Jewish history. The universalist left draws the West's conclusions and remains alert to the dangers of ruling over another people. The traditionalist right draws Judaism's conclusions and remains alert to the dangers of placing the lives of Jews in the hands of other people.

If the State of Israel wants to defend itself from the Muslim majority surrounding it, it must not pull back from Judea and Samaria; but if it wants to defend itself from the prospect of a Muslim majority within it, it must do so. This paradox exists because everyone is correct. The right is correct that a withdrawal from Judea and Samaria would endanger Israel; the left is correct that a continued presence in the territories would endanger Israel. The problem is that since everyone is correct, everyone is also incorrect—and the State of Israel is trapped in an impossible double bind.

7 THE MORAL DILEMMA

The argument over Israel's future is not just an argument about survival. It is an argument about values. For the right, withdrawing from the territories would be both a security danger and an act of Jewish betrayal. For the left, remaining in the territories would be both a demographic danger and an act of moral betrayal.

In the previous chapters I dealt with the dilemmas of survival; here I treat the dilemmas of morality. I shall not touch on the legal status of the territories or the position of international law: this discussion will focus exclusively on questions of humanitarianism and ethics. In the first stage of exploring this dilemma, let us consider the biting criticism of the left over the immorality of Israel's presence in the territories.

THE OCCUPATION CORRUPTS

Democracy is more than majority rule: it is self-rule. A nation in possession of its own democratic nation-state is a nation that governs itself. In dictatorships, the people do not realize their own aspirations—they are subordinated to the aspirations of others. A people under occupation are a people without national freedom, because they are subordinated to the will of another people. Occupation can be defined, therefore, as a type of dictatorship. The only difference between occupation and dictatorship is that in a classical dictatorship the people are subjugated by a single person, whereas in an occupation the people are subjugated by an entire other nation.

In the modern era, the democratic nations of Europe embarked on a worldwide campaign of conquest. They invaded Asia and Africa, subjugating countless nations therein. At home, they governed themselves; abroad, they governed others. Ironically, it was these free European nations who plundered the liberty of others. As the twentieth century went on, that paradox was resolved. The nations of Europe began to roll back their control of Asia and Africa, and the unpleasant anomaly of democracy at home and conquest abroad disappeared. The world was now governed by a new norm: nations that govern themselves do not govern others.

In a surprising and disturbing coincidence, the Six-Day War broke out exactly as the process of European decolonization reached its peak. Ever since that war, Israel has administered a military regime over a civilian population. The State of Israel is a democracy, and it represents the fulfillment of the Jewish people's ancient dream for national freedom—but since 1967, Israel has not simply been realizing its own aspirations for liberty; it has also been robbing the freedom of another people. Since 1967, Israel has been marching against the direction of history.

A BRIEF HISTORY OF THE OCCUPATION

Until the Oslo Accords, Israel's military rule over the civilian population in the territories was almost absolute. The Israeli army served as a police force, patrolling inside Arab towns. One of the army's tasks was to deprive the local population of any possibility of national self-expression. Soldiers serving in the territories were ordered to tear down Palestinian flags and arrest children caught scribbling nationalist graffiti. The Civil Administration was responsible for the day-to-day needs of the civilian population, and dealt with questions of electricity, water, sewage, and transportation for the occupied Palestinian population.

Many Israelis assumed that the Palestinians would reconcile themselves to the new situation because their economy, health care, and education had all improved since the Six-Day War. The Israelis had connected the Palestinians to electricity grids and modern water networks, and had given them access to advanced health care systems. Since the Palestinians' quality of life had improved under Israeli rule, ran the argument, there was no reason for them to resist that rule. But the First Intifada debunked this theory. The broad popular resistance was an expression of decades of accumulated Palestinian rage against Israeli rule. The Palestinians coveted freedom from Israeli rule more than they coveted its economic benefits.

The Palestinian uprising shook Israeli society and propelled it onto a painful trajectory that culminated in the Oslo Accords. These agreements established Palestinian autonomy over parts of the territories, enabling the Arabs to exercise partial self-rule. The framework for partial autonomy was meant to last five years, ending with the signing of a final-status agreement. The

Palestinians expected that they would move from partial to full self-rule after those five years: from autonomy to statehood. The plan was set in action, but it broke down along the way. The Palestinians gained autonomy but not a state; they were left with partial autonomy over a portion of the territories. As a result of the Oslo process, Israel's military control over the Palestinians was minimized, but it never disappeared.

The State of Israel controls all the territory surrounding the enclaves governed by the Palestinian Authority. Palestinian self-rule applies within the specific territory assigned to the Authority, and development or growth is dependent on Israeli authorization. The towns themselves are under Palestinian self-government, but Palestinians must travel on roads under Israeli control whenever they want to visit neighboring towns. The IDF can decide on which roads the Palestinians may or may not travel. In times of heightened security tensions, certain roads in the territories serve Jews only. Sometimes the IDF imposes a closure on Palestinian towns for security reasons and prevents Palestinians from entering and exiting. Most of the time, it must be noted, Palestinian towns are not under closure, and most roads remain open to Palestinian traffic—but this is only because the IDF has decided to keep them open.

That is the crux of the matter: even when the Palestinians enjoy freedom of movement on roads in the territories, their freedom comes not at their own discretion but at that of Israel, which rules over them. The fact that freedom of movement must be granted by the ruler only highlights the dependency of the ruled. Even after the establishment of Palestinian autonomy, key aspects of the Palestinians' daily lives remain out of their hands.

Additionally, while most of the Palestinians live in territory governed by the Palestinian Authority, tens if not hundreds of thousands live outside it, under Israel's direct military rule. The territories, therefore, maintain different degrees of occupation: while most of the Palestinians live under indirect military rule, a sizable minority still lives under direct rule.

Moreover, Israel has planted hundreds of Jewish settlements across the territories it captured in the Six-Day War.[1] These settlements have their own security needs, which sometimes require limiting Palestinians' freedom of movement. This is just one example of moral turpitude arising from Jewish settlement in the territories. Two classes of people inhabit the same land: citizens of the nation that is controlling, and subjects of the nation being controlled.[2] An occupation is defined as military rule over a civilian population, but the IDF is not in the territories only to rule over another civilian population—it is also there to protect its own civilian population.

A DEMOCRATIC OCCUPIER?

The State of Israel is a democracy. It is a polity in which the Israeli people govern themselves. In the territories, however, there is no democracy. The inhabitants of the territories are controlled by another nation, one that *does* govern itself. This dissonance amplifies the moral problem. For if Israel is a democracy, then every citizen must be a full participant in its political power—and if that political power is exploited to occupy another nation, then it follows that every Israeli citizen has an equal share in the military rule over the Palestinians.

One of the left's traditional slogans has been that the occupation corrupts. What the left means is that Israel's policing activities in the territories have a detrimental effect on the character of the citizens who are sent to conduct them. A reserve soldier in the territories who finds himself acting arrogantly and even obscenely toward civilians cannot change this behavior when he returns home. The occupation, Israelis are told repeatedly, is causing Israel to turn into a society of corrupted individuals.

I do not know whether this psychological theory holds water. But as a description it misses and even conceals the real heart of the moral issue. The primary problem is not that the occupation begets corruption, but that the occupation is itself corrupt. The essence of the occupation is that one nation deprives another nation of its liberty. Since the nation in charge is a democracy, every single citizen shares moral responsibility for this policy. The occupation does not lead to a loss of morality—the occupation itself is immoral.

In response to the moral argument against Israel's military presence in the territories, it is common to hear the retort "But they want to kill us." It is also said that if Israel withdraws from the territories and ends the occupation, Israelis might be acting morally—but they would also be dead. These are arguments about security; they are important and even constitute moral arguments in their own right. I addressed them methodically and at length earlier. In those earlier discussions, I demonstrated that some make the opposite case about survival, arguing that it is Israel's continued presence in the territories that most threatens the Jewish state. But might there also be a non-security answer to the left's powerful and persuasive ethical case against the occupation?

PERHAPS THERE IS NO OCCUPATION?

Are Judea and Samaria occupied? Logically, for a territory to be defined as occupied, two conditions must be satisfied: someone must be doing the occupying and something must be being occupied.[3] Israel invaded and conquered Judea and Samaria in the Six-Day War and has held the territory ever since. This is the basic case for saying that Israel is an occupier. But what is being occupied? On the face of it, the answer is Jordan. Judea and Samaria were in Jordanian hands on the eve of the war, and they were forcibly taken by Israel in the course of that war.

At this point, however, we must ask a question that might sound childish, but is in fact critical: Who started the war? Who fired the first shot?

Israel fought on multiple fronts in the Six-Day War. The IDF engaged the Egyptian army in the south, and the Syrian army in the north. Israel was not interested in an additional third front in the east. This is why the government of Prime Minister Levi Eshkol warned King Hussein of Jordan to stay out of the war.[4] But the Jordanian monarch was unable to withstand the pressure from his Arab allies, and he joined the Egyptian and Syrian assault, attacking Israel on day one of the war. The first shots fired across the Jordanian-Israeli border during the 1967 war were the Jordanian shelling of Israeli civilian population centers in West Jerusalem. Jordan, however, made a mistake: its entry into the war did not lead to Israel's collapse but to its expansion. At the end of the war, Israel found itself with East Jerusalem in its hands, as well as the Judean Desert and the hills of Samaria. This much is an indisputable historical fact: Judea and Samaria were conquered not in an act of Israeli aggression but in an act of Israeli defense.

Would it have been appropriate for Israel to return the territories seized from Jordan when defending against Jordanian aggression? To turn the question on its head: Was an aggressor state entitled to demand back the territory it had lost as a consequence of its aggression? The answer to these questions, I believe, is clear. A world in which aggression bears no cost is a dangerous world indeed, because it is a world in which bullies face no risks. A hostile power defeated in a war that it has initiated is clearly not entitled to overturn the results of that war.[5]

Another strong reason can be adduced to refute the historical premise that Judea and Samaria were rightfully Jordanian territory. This territory first fell into Jordan's hands during Israel's War of Independence through an earlier act of Jordanian aggression. The territory was supposed to have become part of a Palestinian state; this is why most of the world, with the exception of Pakistan and the United Kingdom, refused to recognize Jordan's annexation of it. Judea and Samaria thus constitute territory that the Jordanians conquered in an act of unjustified aggression and also lost through an act of unjustified aggression.

There was no conceivable moral reason or ethical justification for Israel to return the territories to Jordan. Even so, the Israeli government decided several days after the end of the war, on 19 June 1967, that it was willing to return most of the territory captured in the war to the neighboring Arab states in exchange for a peace treaty. The State of Israel, as Defense Minister Moshe Dayan said, was "waiting for a phone call" from King Hussein.[6] But the telephone never rang. Israel received its answer instead from the Arab League summit in Khartoum, which delivered a blunt and unambiguous reply. This was the famous Three Noes response to Israel's offer: no peace with Israel, no negotiations with Israel, no recognition of Israel. In short, Israel holds Judea and Samaria at present because of a wanton act of Jordanian aggression compounded by a unilateral act of Arab rejectionism.

Returning to the original question, in order to define land as being under occupation, we must start with the assumption that there was a historic moment in which it was first occupied. But Judea and Samaria were never occupied through an act of aggression by Israel. They were captured from the Jordanians because of Jordan's aggression, and they remained in Israeli hands because of Arab rejectionism. And if no land exists that can be justifiably claimed as occupied, in this line of argument, there is no occupation either.

But what if the Jordanians are not the injured parties?[7] Perhaps the mountains of Judea and Samaria should be defined as occupied territory because they were stolen from the Palestinian people who live there?

Never in history has there been a Palestinian state, but such a state *could* have come into existence.[8] It was first offered to the Arabs of Mandatory Palestine by the British government in 1937. At the height of a wave of violent Arab riots, the British dispatched a Royal Commission headed by Lord Peel to look into the conflict; the commission concluded that the solution was to partition the land into two states. Under the Peel Partition Plan, the Palestinian Arabs could have received approximately 75 percent of the landmass of Mandatory Palestine, and the Jews would have received the remaining quarter.

Despite the shrunken dimensions of the territory offered to the Jews, the Zionist leadership headed by David Ben-Gurion and Chaim Weizmann accepted the principle of partition. The Arabs, however, led by the Mufti Haj Amin al-Husseini, rejected the proposal outright.[9] The partition plan fell off the international agenda, and returned to relevance ten years later with minor revisions. When the British handed over the task of determining the future of the Holy Land to the United Nations, the organization sent its own committee of inquiry—the United Nations Special Committee on Palestine, or UNSCOP—to explore the land and decide its fate.

Similarly to the Peel Commission, UNSCOP reached the conclusion that the land must be divided into two states. The commissioners presented their conclusions to the U.N. General Assembly, recommending that some 55 percent of the land come under Jewish sovereignty while the remaining 45 percent would fall under Arab sovereignty.[10] The United Nations held a vote on the proposal on 29 November 1947, endorsing partition. In a repeat of history, the Jews responded in the affirmative and welcomed the proposal, while the Arabs—yet again—answered, "No."

Nowadays, many people around the world imagine that the Palestinians lack a state because their land was occupied by Israel in an act of war. But no Palestinian state was ever occupied, because no such state has ever existed. And the reason that no Palestinian state has ever existed is that the Palestinians have rejected repeated offers that would have enabled the establishment of such a state. The Palestinians' objection to the establishment of a state for the Jews led them to refuse the establishment of a sovereign state for themselves. It is an undeniable historical fact that the Palestinians are a people without a country. It is also an undeniable historical fact that the reason is not Israeli aggression but Palestinian rejectionism.

The rejectionism that was born in 1937 and resurfaced in 1947 has never disappeared. In 2001, Israeli Prime Minister Ehud Barak offered PLO Chairman Yasser Arafat a Palestinian state. Arafat refused, and two months later the Second Intifada erupted. During the course of the intifada, President Bill Clinton proposed an even more far-reaching framework known as the Clinton Parameters. The Barak government agreed; the Palestinians refused. Clinton observed that Arafat's rejectionism would lead the peace process to a dead end.[11] Indeed, as the great Israeli statesman Abba Eban said, the Palestinians never miss an opportunity to miss an opportunity.[12]

The Palestinians were then presented with an additional opportunity: seven years later, Prime Minister Ehud Olmert made Palestinian Authority President Mahmoud Abbas an even more generous and wide-ranging offer than Ehud Barak had made at Camp David. But Abbas left Olmert without an answer and the conflict without a resolution.[13] The tragic reality is that the stateless Palestinians are victims of their own rejectionism. In another memorable aphorism, Eban compared the Palestinians to a child who, after killing his parents, pleads for mercy as an orphan.

The complex history of Judea and Samaria only complicates the territories' status further. This is land that was intended, with the Zionists' agreement, to become part of a Palestinian state in 1947—but Palestinian rejectionism meant that it was swallowed up by Jordan in one war and remained in Israeli hands after their capture by Israel in another war. This is not occupied territory. The most appropriate definition for these territories is that they are disputed.

SO IS THERE OR IS THERE NOT AN OCCUPATION?

Let us apply this logic in full. On one hand, the territories are not stolen land that came under Israel's control by immoral means, so they are not in themselves occupied. On the other, as we have seen, Israel imposes military rule on a Palestinian population that has no say over the state's decisions, so the Palestinians are a nation that lives *under* occupation. The conclusion is that the territories are not occupied, but the Palestinian people *are*.

This situation is what confounds Israeli discussions of the status of Judea and Samaria. Both the left and right are correct. The left is correct about the people and the right is correct about the land. Listen carefully and sensitively to the left, and you will hear that leftists are talking almost exclusively about the Palestinians living under Israeli occupation. Listen carefully and sensitively to the Israeli right, and you will hear that right-wingers are talking almost exclusively about territory that was never unjustly occupied. The left makes unconscious inferences from the people to the land; the right makes unconscious inferences from the land to the people. Since both sides are correct, they are also both mistaken, and neither can express the full complexity of the situation: the people in the territories live under occupation, even though the land on which they live is not itself occupied.

8 THE JEWISH DILEMMA

THE RELIGIOUS ARGUMENT

The religious right believes that settling the Land of Israel is a divine commandment and withdrawing from the Land of Israel is a sin. This religious argument allies with the security argument as follows: a withdrawal from Judea and Samaria would not only endanger the Jewish people, it would also violate Jewish law. The religious argument adds gravity to the security argument and turns the notion of withdrawal from a mere mistake into a cardinal sin.

Where is it written that settling the land is a commandment? The primary source for this proposition is the clear pronouncement of the great medieval Jewish scholar Nachmanides. He averred that the commandment of settlement should be included in the list of 613 biblical commandments:

> Since we were commanded to inherit the land that God Almighty gave our forefathers—Abraham, Isaac, and Jacob—we must neither leave it in the hands of another nation nor leave it desolate. For God told them, "You shall take posses-

sion of the land and settle in it, for I have given you the land to possess, and you shall inherit the land" . . . and this is what the sages call "war by commandment."[1]

Nachmanides teaches that there is a biblical commandment to settle the Land of Israel as well as a prohibition against ceding it to foreign nations: "We must [not] leave it in the hands of another nation."

In Jewish law, however, it is also expressly forbidden to fulfill a commandment at the cost of endangering human life. Consider Maimonides' clear and decisive position on violating the Sabbath in order to save a life:

> It is forbidden to delay desecrating the Sabbath for a person who is dangerously ill, as it is said [Leviticus 18:5]: "and Mine ordinances, which if a man do, he shall live by them," i.e. and not by [My ordinances]. Learn that the laws of the Torah only exist in the world of mercy, loving kindness, and peace in the world."[2]

What if a person wishes to sacrifice himself to fulfill a biblical injunction of his own free will and out of profound religious devotion? Maimonides' answer to such a person is severe: "He sins and rebels through his deeds, his blood is on his own head, and he forfeits his own life. As Almighty God says, 'If a man keeps My ordinances, he shall live by them, not die by them.'" Maimonides is explicit that one who sacrifices himself for the sake of the Torah is in fact rebelling against the Torah.

It follows that if the commandment of settlement were, in theory, a danger to human life, then adherence to this commandment would not be a fulfillment of religious law but a violation of it. Indeed, so judged the late Rabbi Ovadia Yosef—formerly Israel's Sephardic chief rabbi, and founder and spiritual leader of the ultra-Orthodox Shas Party. He ruled that if it transpired that a withdrawal from parts of the Land of Israel would bring security and save human lives, then not only would a withdrawal be permitted under religious law, it would be obligatory.

It seems that everyone agrees that it is permitted to return territories from the Land of Israel for the sake of achieving this goal [peace], for no commandment stands in the way of saving a life. This is like the question of whether a sick person may be fed on Yom Kippur, when the expert doctor, even if he is a Gentile, is the one to determine the patient's situation. Should the doctor say that there is a danger to the sick person's life from fasting, or that his health might deteriorate and this would endanger him, then the sick person should be fed. . . .

The same applies to our situation: If the army's top commanders, together with the statesmen who are empowered to decide, determine that lives would be saved by violating the commandment against returning territory, we are meant to trust them and allow them to return the territory. If there is a disagreement between doctors about whether a patient would be endangered by fasting on Yom Kippur—such as if two say he needs to eat but a hundred say he does not—the patient should be fed, since we err on the side of saving lives.

Such is the law here. If there is disagreement on the matter, and some experts say it is not a matter of saving lives, but others say that there is a fear of immediate war and the loss of lives if the territories are not returned, we err on the side of saving lives, and the territories must be returned to avert the possibility of war.[3]

Rabbi Ovadia Yosef's position, however, is not the only relevant perspective on religious law. The Yesha Rabbis—a coalition of hardline settlement rabbis—ruled that there was an absolute prohibition on pulling back from parts of the Land of Israel and transferring them to Arab hands, and that complicity in such a withdrawal was also a violation of the Torah:

> The accord that the government has signed with the terrorists [the Oslo Accords] totally contradicts Jewish law in two senses: a) It is forbidden to relinquish part of the Land of Israel to the hands of Gentiles, and certainly not to those who hate us and want to annihilate us; b) The prohibition "thou shalt not stand idly by the blood of thy neighbor" (Leviticus 19:16). The IDF's withdrawal from cities and military camps in Judea and Samaria endangers the Jews who live in Judea and Samaria, and those who live in nearby towns along the Green Line, and it is forbidden in the Torah to stand by when somebody is in danger, and it is all the more forbidden to actively endanger them.
>
> This premise, that the IDF's withdrawal from the cities and military camps of Judea and Samaria constitutes a danger, is accepted by military experts, and has even been expressed by officers serving in the field. . . . We declare that the IDF's withdrawal from Judea and Samaria, and the vacating of military camps, posts, and other places, is indeed against

Jewish law for the aforementioned reasons: the prohibition on relinquishing territory in the Land of Israel to foreign rule and the prohibition "thou shalt not stand idly by the blood of thy neighbor."[4]

The ruling that the evacuation of settlements is a violation of the Torah rests on two religious arguments. The first is a prohibition on transferring parts of the Land of Israel to Gentiles, rooted in the writings of Nachmanides; the second is the prohibition on endangering human life. These arguments complement each other in the rabbinic ruling, but we cannot infer from them that it is permissible to endanger human life for the sake of settling the Land of Israel.

In reality, therefore, there is no fundamental legal dispute between Rabbi Ovadia Yosef and the Yesha Rabbis. Rabbi Ovadia ruled that *if* a withdrawal averts a danger to human life, *then* a withdrawal is obligatory in Jewish law; the Yesha Rabbis ruled that *since* a withdrawal would endanger human life, *then* a withdrawal is forbidden. The theoretical debate is without substance: it is not about the importance of human life in religious law, but only about the practical question of how best to protect human life.

This convoluted religious dispute was best elucidated by Rabbi Hayim David HaLevi:

In sum, there is no clearly enumerated law from which we can prove that a withdrawal from the liberated territories of the Land of Israel in the framework of peace negotiations with our neighbors is prohibited by law. . . . The decisive consideration in this case is the existence and security of the nation. An Israeli government, therefore, that concludes that relinquishing the territories would avert war and bloodshed and would usher in a true peace is entitled and even obligated to do so. In contrast, a withdrawal that would be likely to cause a security threat is totally forbidden.[5]

The previous chapters concerned the compelling argument that a withdrawal from Judea and Samaria would bring disaster, as well as the equally compelling argument that remaining in Judea and Samaria would bring disaster. A withdrawal might indeed endanger human life, but refraining from a withdrawal might also endanger human life. Since the protection of human life has supreme importance in Jewish law, outweighing all other possible considerations, we must conclude that if a decision to withdraw from the territories were the right decision from a security perspective, then it must also be the right decision from the perspective of Jewish law. But if a decision to *remain* in the territories were the right decision from a security perspective, then *this* would also be the right decision from the perspective of Jewish law. The argument concerning religious law does not run parallel to the argument concerning security—it is a product of that security argument.

No ruling based exclusively on religious law could determine the fate of Judea and Samaria. In matters of life and death, Jewish law decrees that considerations of religious law cannot trump considerations of security. On the contrary, considerations of security are the necessary factual basis for any religious determination. It follows that the argument that a territorial withdrawal would not only endanger the Jewish people but violate Jewish law is fundamentally unsound under the very logic of Jewish religious law. A more precise formulation would be that *if* a withdrawal endangered the Jewish people, *then* it would violate Jewish law; but if *remaining* in Judea and Samaria endangered the Jewish people, then *this* would violate Jewish law. In conclusion, the religious argument does not complement the security argument—it is derived from it.

THE NATIONALIST ARGUMENT

The author A. B. Yehoshua has described Judaism in terms of a surprising and perceptive metaphor: Judaism is a hermaphrodite. A hermaphrodite is a person who has both male and female reproductive organs—who is both a man and a woman. What could this metaphor allude to? Judaism is both a religion and a nation. It has all the characteristics of a religion: holy scriptures, belief in the divine, and sacred rituals. At the same time, it also has all the characteristics of a nation: collective memories, a historic homeland, a common tongue, and a strong and profound sense of communal solidarity. Both a religion and a nation.

From the perspective of religious law, as we have seen, the right's argument for remaining in the territories is weak. Religious law cannot lend additional weight to other, practical arguments. Despite that, the right still has in its reserves a powerful and weighty argument derived from the other pillar of Judaism's bifurcated ideology—the national pillar.

The national organism, like any other living organism, has both a body and a soul. This is how people thought about nationhood in nineteenth-century Europe. A nation's soul is expressed through its culture; its body is its land. The soul of the Italian nation finds expression in the creations of Dante and da Vinci, but its body is the soil of Italy. The soul of the French nation is visible in the creations of Pascal and Descartes, but its body is the soil of France.

The soul of the Jewish people can be discerned in the Hebrew Bible and the Talmud, in the *Zohar* and in centuries of Jewish philosophy. But its body is the Land of Israel. Hebron, Bethlehem, and Shiloh do not "belong" to the Jewish people—they are an inseparable part of the Jewish people. One's location does not just account for *where* one is but *who* one is. Man, wrote the great Hebrew poet Shaul Tchernichovsky, is "nothing but the image of his native landscape."[6] One's homeland is not simply the place one was born, but a part of oneself.

A nation's land is part of its identity. Nations with a healthy national consciousness feel no need to justify their ownership of their homeland, just as people never feel the need to justify ownership of their own bodies. As Jabotinsky put it: "Ask a French farmer such a question, whether France is his land! . . . These are axioms, not 'riddles.' Only these pitiful figures, with their Diaspora psyche, have turned this axiom into a 'riddle' that needs to be investigated and 'solved.'" If a nation's homeland is part of its identity, then to cede a part of the Jewish homeland is to cede a part of Jewish identity.[7]

Jewish identity contains an inbuilt tension: it is an expression of both a religion and a nationality. During the Exile, Judaism was primarily a religion; Zionism's great achievement was to awaken the national spirit of the bifurcated Jewish identity from its ancient slumber. A withdrawal from Judea and Samaria would be a blow to Zionist identity because it would be an admission that Judaism is not a healthy nationality, but rather a lightweight religious culture. For Judaism, the main problem in renouncing Judea and Samaria stems not from religious law but from national identity.

THE PROPHETIC ARGUMENT

The spirit of prophecy is an organic part of the Jewish religion. The ancient prophets of Israel all preached their own visions, demanding that the Jewish people build a new world, a world radically different from its pagan past. The pagan world worshipped power, believing that power itself was divine and that whoever held power was similarly godlike. The prophets of Israel dreamt of changing the world. They sought to transform a world that attached religious significance to power into a world that attached religious significance to restraints on power. Rejecting a world where the strong controlled the weak, they longed to create one in which the strong would be commanded to discover empathy and compassion toward the weak.

The Zionist movement faced precisely this Jewish test of the majority's relationship with minorities. It was David Ben-Gurion who identified the test: "No truly Jewish state will ever rise, large or small, over part of the land or the whole of it, unless the homeland of the prophets realizes the great and eternal moral aspirations that we have borne in our hearts and souls for generations: one law for citizen and stranger alike. . . . The Jewish state will be an example to the world in its behavior toward minorities and foreigners."[8]

The Jewish people's return to the land of the prophets must also mark their return to the vision of the prophets; an Israeli society hoping to fulfill the biblical prophecies must be judged on its relationship with minorities, foreigners, and the other.[9] The relationship between the State of Israel and the Arabs who live under its control grants Israelis an opportunity to fulfill the biblical vision, but it also confronts them with a challenge at which they could fail. Israel's decades-long military rule over a civilian population since the Six-Day War represents a religious failure. The prophets' vision of a strong society remaining sensitive toward the weak is betrayed anew every day by the IDF's policing activities at checkpoints across the territories.

Withdrawing from the territories subverts Israel's national identity, on the one hand, but remaining there violates the vision of the prophets, on the other. In the previous chapter, I concluded that the territories were not occupied but the people who lived in them were nonetheless under occupation. We have just seen that the Land of Israel is part of Jewish identity, but the occupation of the Palestinians who reside there gnaws away at the purpose of that Jewish identity.

AN INTRA-BIBLICAL TENSION

The book of Genesis tells the story of the patriarch Abraham, who hears a voice, departs from Mesopotamia, and journeys to the Land of Israel. The book of Exodus tells the story of his descendants, who hear a voice, depart from Egypt, and journey to the Land of Israel. The Hebrew Bible dreams that the Jewish people will enter the Land of Israel and settle it; and it threatens the Jewish people with exile. The Bible warns repeatedly that if the Jewish people sin, they will be exiled from their land. This is the central organizing principle of the biblical narrative. The Land of Israel is the heart of the biblical story. This is why it is impossible to detract from the importance of the Land of Israel without detracting from the importance of the Hebrew Bible.

The Bible does not just tell a story, it also enumerates laws—and some of those laws have a clear rationale and basis. The rationale that is most frequently repeated and tied to many laws is sensitivity toward foreigners. Why is it important to care for the weak in society, including foreigners? "Because you were foreigners in the Land of Egypt." Israelis must exercise social sensitivity toward foreigners because they too were once foreigners. "Foreigners" (*gerim* in Hebrew) in the biblical sense are not necessarily citizens of foreign countries. A foreigner is simply a member of a minority—a person without political protection, who belongs outside mainstream society. A foreigner is anyone who can be easily exploited and abused.

The Hebrew Bible is a combination of narrative and law. The dominant motif of the biblical story is the connection to the Land of Israel; the dominant motif of the biblical commandments is sensitivity to foreigners. How interesting and how ironic that in Israel's present reality these two motifs are in constant collision. Judea and Samaria are the undisputed heart of the biblical Land of Israel. They harbor the most ancient of the Jewish people's historical memories. This is the land where the patriarchs roamed. This is where the bulk of the biblical drama unfolded. But these same hills are also home to a civilian population under Israeli military rule. Sensitivity toward foreigners requires that Israel withdraw from the territories, but devotion to the Land of Israel requires that Israel settle them. History has fated these two biblical motifs to face off against each other, and this poses a challenge to anyone who aspires to fulfill the vision of the Bible in the land of the Bible.

This trap for Judaism is also a trap for Zionism. In *Altneuland*, the magnum opus of the Zionist visionary Theodor Herzl, one of the characters, Steineck, says that the right to statehood is the right of every single nation: "Everyone deserves a homeland."[10] It was in the name of this universal right that the early Zionists demanded the political liberation of the Jewish people. But if Zionism is a national liberation movement, does it not contradict itself when it subjugates another nation?

The problem, of course, is that by the same token we could also ask the inverse question: If Zionism is the movement to restore the Jewish people to their historic homeland, does it not contradict itself by relinquishing parts of the land of its forefathers and foremothers? Zionism is the Jewish national liberation movement, but it is also the movement to restore the Jewish people to their ancient homeland. The situation forged by the Six-Day War pits two foundational pillars of Judaism against each other—and pits two foundational pillars of Zionism against each other as well.

ISRAELIS ARE TRAPPED

When it comes to Judea and Samaria, the Jewish people are trapped. The Zionist trap exacerbates the Jewish trap, which aligns with the moral dilemma, and both feed into the trap of brute survival. Israel's presence in the territories both fulfills Zionism and contradicts Zionism. A territorial withdrawal would both fulfill the prophetic vision of Judaism and undermine the national expression of Judaism. Control of the territories both protects Israel geographically and threatens it demographically. It turns out that everyone is right, and since everyone is right—all are trapped.

9 FROM CONFUSION TO UNDERSTANDING

Not all Israelis feel confused. Some on the Israeli right believe that Israel would not endanger itself by holding on to the territories. In their minds, the demographic and moral dangers involved in remaining in the territories do not imperil the country's future—everything will be fine. Oftentimes, this sense of personal security has religious roots. The God of Israel, they believe, who delivered this land to the Jewish people in a miraculous war, will continue to defend them as long as they defend the land.

There are also some on the Israeli left who believe that Israel would not endanger itself by withdrawing from the territories. To their minds, the barbaric chaos engulfing the Middle East would neither submerge the territories vacated by the IDF nor spill over from those territories into Israel itself. Oftentimes, this sense of personal security is rooted in faith in the international community. After all, Israel would demand security guarantees from the international community as part of a peace accord, and these arrangements would defend Israel from any dangers that might follow a withdrawal.

But most Israelis struggle with entrusting the keys to their security to the hands of either the God of Israel or the nations of the world. Across the Diaspora, the Jews in their various communities never developed the means and mechanisms to defend themselves. They entrusted their security to the hands of the Gentiles who ruled them, believing that they were thereby expressing their faith and trust in God. The result, as we know, was catastrophe. Zionism drew some stark lessons from Jewish history. Zionists inferred that neither blind faith in the Gentiles nor blind faith in God would guarantee security. Zionism is the belief that the Jews can trust only themselves and can rely only on themselves.

Nobody who accepts this lesson of history, as the early Zionists did, can believe that Israel should either risk relinquishing territory out of trust in international guarantees or risk holding on to that territory out of trust in God. This is the fundamental basis of the great political confusion afflicting Israel today.

THREE RESPONSES TO ISRAELIS' CONFUSION

Israelis' despair about the prospects for peace has led to a more general despair within sectors of the Israeli peace camp. An Israel that no longer believes in peace is an Israel in which the more radical fringes of the peace camp can no longer believe either. The abandonment of the peace process has provoked the radical wing of the Israeli left to despair of Zionism altogether.

A similar process has unfolded on the Israeli right. The religious right waged a campaign against the Disengagement from Gaza but found itself alone. Right-wingers were terrified to discover that most Israelis supported the Disengagement Plan. Some sectors of the religious right also despaired of the Israeli people. A similar feeling crept into the radical wing of the Israeli right: Israelis who no longer believe in the Land of Israel are Israelis in whom the radical right can no longer believe.

The polar ends of the two camps have lost faith in Zionism, and they despair of Israel altogether.

But there has also been a third reaction to Israel's crisis of political ideas. This is the reaction of the many Israelis who have no interest in ruling over the Palestinians but equally would not dare endanger themselves by pulling out of the territories. These Israelis have found themselves at an impasse. If Israelis remain in the territories, they could be torn to shreds by the occupation, but if they leave the territories, they could be overrun by a terror no less violent.

So what do they do? The answer came in the summer of 2011 when tens of thousands of Israelis took to the streets, pitched tents, and declared, "The people demand social justice!"

For decades, the Arab-Israeli conflict had held a monopoly over political passion in Israel. Campaigns in support of diplomatic accords or in opposition to territorial withdrawals had brought tens of thousands of citizens to the streets, while social campaigns had left the apathetic majority at home. In the summer of 2011, the situation changed. The tremendous social energy that erupted during those protests proved that the conflict had lost its monopoly. As long as the dreams of a land united or a land at peace filled Israelis' political consciousness, their social consciousness slumbered. But the disintegration of the big ideas cleared room for the emergence of a new social awareness. Unlike the way the two extremes reacted, most Israelis have not given up on their country. The collapse of the big ideas provoked not a collapse of idealism but a transferal of political energy to new horizons.

The collapse of the right's dream of a Greater Israel and left's dream of peace should have produced broad national agreement in Israel. But this never happened. Instead, Israel's political discourse became uglier and more vitriolic. It now deals more with personalities than ideas, with insults more than ideologies. The aggressive, personal, and invective nature of public discourse is not a product of ideological polarization, but of the implosion of the ideological poles. In the absence of meaningful differences on values, all that remains is the accentuation of differences between personalities. Israel's political discourse is degenerating not because Israelis have moved apart from one another but precisely because they have been drawn closer to one another.

Politics is no longer the field in which Israelis express their positions. Politics has turned into the field in which they affirm their identities. Political discourse no longer pits idea against idea, but tribe against tribe. When politics ceases to rely on arguments and stops offering ideas, all it can do is channel identities. So it was that the disintegration of the ideas of the left and right, and the collapse of their traditional ideologies, did not abolish the rift between the two camps—they aggravated it.

FROM IDEOLOGICAL TO TRIBAL POLITICS

One of the greatest threats to any person's ability to listen is groupthink. John Stuart Mill, one of the leading thinkers in Western liberalism, recognized that people are generally inclined to lose their sense of doubt when they affiliate with groups that echo their opinions back at them: "People . . . place the same unbounded reliance only on such of their opinions as are shared by all who surround them, or to whom they habitually defer: for in proportion to a man's want of confidence in his own solitary judgment, does he usually repose, with implicit trust, on the infallibility of 'the world' in general. And the world, to each individual, means the part of it with which he comes in contact."[1]

This penetrating insight by an English philosopher in the nineteenth century goes some way toward explaining the problems of Israel's national conversation in the twenty-first. The conviction of our own beliefs does not depend on the reasonableness of our arguments but on the strength of our identification with a group that professes those beliefs. Even those who are personally aware that they can sometimes be wrong subconsciously deny that their *group* could also be wrong. In other words, when the sphere of public discourse is no longer a place where ideas meet but an arena where tribes clash, critical thinking is in danger.

I can personally attest to the almost obsessive need to bring opinions in line with group identity. Whenever I speak in public about liberalism and humanism, I am immediately suspected of being a leftist. Whenever I speak about patriotism and Zionism, I am immediately suspected of being a right-winger. A close friend, who does not wear a kippa, tells me that whenever he waxes lyrical about the wisdom of the Talmud, people suspect that he is about to become religious. The right's monopoly on the image of Zionism, the left's monopoly on the image of humanism, and religious society's monopoly on the image of Judaism all hurt Israelis' ability to think about Zionism, humanism, and Judaism objectively. When people fail to judge beliefs by their own reasonableness but instead view them according to the sectarian identity of their adherents, we can conclude that crowd psychology has replaced independent thought.

This is the great missed opportunity of Israel's political discourse: instead of provoking humility and mutual listening, the collapse of ideologies has provoked the closing of ranks and mutual recriminations.

In this book I focus on the fractured conversation between Jews and Jews, but even this less than ideal conversation is far better than the conversation between Jews and Palestinians.

THE FRACTURED JEWISH-PALESTINIAN CONVERSATION

Since the birth of Zionism, many Palestinians have seen it as a colonialist movement. In the Palestinians' eyes, Western civilization constitutes a single destructive empire extending its tentacles into the Middle East—and one of its most devastating tentacles is Zionism. This is how the Palestinian National Charter defines Zionism:

> Zionism is a political movement organically associated with international imperialism and antagonistic to all action for liberation and to progressive movements in the world. . . . Israel is the instrument of the Zionist movement, and geographical base for world imperialism placed strategically in the midst of the Arab homeland to combat the hopes of the Arab nation for liberation, unity, and progress.[2]

This perception finds a certain justification in the statements of some of the early Zionists, who initially conceived of a Jewish state as a force for extending the borders of Europe into Asia.[3] The Zionists, in this narrative, were the emissaries of the British Empire, and when the imperial hegemon began to falter, they struck an alliance with the American empire instead. For many Palestinians, the confrontation with Israel is a confrontation with a world power that is greater than Israel.[4]

At the same time, many Israelis feel that their confrontation with the Palestinians is a confrontation with a historic force that is greater than the Palestinians. They feel that the violence wrought against them has a broader historical context, and specifically that it is an expression of anti-Semitism. The dark energy that once abounded among Europeans now abounds among Palestinians. This feeling is nourished by, among other factors, the Palestinians' own adoption of classic anti-Semitic myths. The Hamas Covenant, for example, which speaks for a mood prevalent among Palestinians, says this about the Jews:

> With their money, they took control of the world media, news agencies, the press, publishing houses, broadcasting stations, and others. With their money they stirred revolutions in various parts of the world with the purpose of achieving their interests and reaping the fruit therein. They were behind the French Revolution, the Communist revolution and most of the revolutions we heard and hear about, here and there. . . . With their money they were able to control imperialistic countries and instigate them to colonize many countries in order to enable them to exploit their resources and spread corruption there.

They obtained the Balfour Declaration, formed the League of Nations through which they could rule the world. They were behind World War II, through which they made huge financial gains by trading in armaments, and paved the way for the establishment of their state. It was they who instigated the replacement of the League of Nations with the United Nations and the Security Council to enable them to rule the world through them.[5]

The anti-Semitic conspiracy theories born in Europe have found a new home in the heart of the Palestinian resistance. The myths are the same myths. The anti-Semitism, many Israelis fear, is the same anti-Semitism.

Palestinians face Israelis and see in them European colonialism; Israelis face Palestinians and see in them European anti-Semitism. Each side sees the other as representing Europe in its ugliest and most threatening guise. Each side sees the other as the product of a broader phenomenon of which it itself is a victim. In the Palestinians' narrative, they are the victims of Israel. In the Israelis' narrative, they are the victims of the Palestinians. In this conflict, each side is the victim of its own victims.

This is one of the reasons why conversation between them is so battered and wounded.[6] Psychologically, victims cannot exercise empathy for their aggressors; so when both sides see themselves as victims, empathy necessarily disappears and understanding moves ever farther away.

Can the Jewish-Palestinian conversation be healed? If a path to listening and understanding can be found, it may well be through religion. When Tony Blair was elected prime minister of the United Kingdom, he rolled up his sleeves and set out to help the warring parties in Northern Ireland to reach understandings. When asked why he thought he would succeed where so many before him had failed, Blair answered that he knew something others did not: religion is not just part of the problem; it can be part of the solution.[7] How could religion, which cultivates fanaticism, sows violence, and widens the gulf between Israelis and Palestinians, also serve as a bridge between them?

One fruitful answer can be found on the ground. At an interfaith event in Jerusalem in summer 2016, in the foothills of Mount Zion, Jewish and Muslim religious figures gathered to sing songs of praise in unison to the one and only God of Abraham.[8] Such a special event should not have been so special: Judaism and Islam have many religious attributes in common. Both faiths believe in a single God, both have a corpus of religious law, and both have a common hero—Abraham, or Ibrahim. One of the event's participants, the philosopher Meir Buzaglo, shared an eye-opening insight with me. Over the past few decades, the notion has taken root that Judaism belongs within a common Judeo-Christian heritage. Buzaglo proposes replacing the Judeo-Christian narrative with a Judeo-Muslim one. Judaism holds more in common with Islam than with Christianity. This insight surprised me. I discovered that it has far-reaching consequences.

The hidden temptation in embracing the Judeo-Christian narrative is that it enables Jews to feel at home in Western culture. But this narrative exacts a heavy price, because while it connects Jews to the West, it also isolates them from the Middle East. The cultivation of a Judeo-Muslim narrative has manifold advantages. If Jews feel that they belong to a narrative that includes Islam, and if Muslims feel that they belong to a narrative that includes Judaism, then a new consciousness might be forged. Nowadays, the stories that Jews and Muslims tell about each other pit them both against each other. In a Judeo-Muslim story, they would stand together, one *with* the other.

Jews cannot be brought to accept the Palestinian narrative, and Palestinians cannot be brought to accept the Israeli narrative, but the two might be able to transcend both narratives to forge a new narrative, greater than the sum of its parts. Religion might help both sides cultivate the climate that could rehabilitate the ability of Jews and Palestinians to listen to each other.[9]

Unfortunately, I must painfully point out the limits of such radical thinking. In practice, religious leaders in Israel today do not use sacred texts to advance understanding, cultivate empathy, or engender a sense of unity of purpose among all the Children of Abraham. In practice, the loudest voices among Muslim religious leaders do not identify Jews as religious or cultural allies. Perhaps in an ideal world, religion could bring people together, but in the present reality, religion tears them apart.

A basic precondition for moving from the present reality to an ideal world is that the mainstream interpretation of religion must change. The late Rabbi Menachem Froman, a pioneer of coexistence, used to say that both Judaism and Islam must discover themselves anew.[10] He clarified that both faiths must undergo regeneration in order to enable each side to understand the other.

Therein lies the weakness of this idea. For religion to change how people perceive reality, people first need to change how they perceive religion. We cannot expect a shift in attitudes to follow from evolving interpretations, because a shift in attitudes is a precondition for interpretations to evolve. This is a vicious cycle of sorts: people must already be tolerant for religion to make them tolerant.

The conversation between Jews and Palestinians is fractured, and the conversation between Jews and Jews is also fractured—but there can be no comparison between the depths of these wounds. As we have seen, there are steep obstacles preventing the use of religion and culture in the service of mutual understanding between Israelis and Palestinians. But the conversation between Jews could be healed with the inspiration of their common culture—primarily the Talmud.

AN UNDERSTANDING HEART

The Talmud is the ultimate source of authority in Jewish religious law. Every religious law that Jews have fulfilled through the generations, and that they continue to fulfill, emerged from and rests on the text of the Talmud. But a casual reader would be surprised to discover that the Talmud does not enumerate the laws that Jews must follow; rather, it records the debates about those laws. The Talmud is unique among tomes of religious law for canonizing not the law itself but disagreements about the law. Discredited legal positions are not part of the practical world of Judaism, but they remain part of its intellectual world. So whereas Jews may not act in accordance with these discredited positions, Jews must still study them and attend to them. Discredited positions remain part of the world of Torah even if they form no part of religious law.

The Talmudic discourse of yesteryear is the opposite of the political discourse of today. In today's political discourse, once people adopt a position from the marketplace of ideas, they stop listening to the positions they have rejected. Oftentimes they even attack those positions and belittle those who hold them. This depressing picture describes not only Israeli political discourse; in recent years, Western publics have also lost their ability to listen. Liberals in the United States think of conservatives precisely the same way conservatives think of liberals. Each side looks at the other and sees a mob of dangerous people who profess immoral beliefs that threaten the core values of the whole of society.

Social media networks only aggravate this problem. Complex or nuanced comments do not go viral. The method behind social media is to amplify the blunt and oppositional, and thus to incentivize a style of writing that demonizes the other side and silences any curiosity about it. In the current climate, any opinion that we do not choose to hear is removed from our sphere of interest.

The Talmudic mode of discourse raises questions for the Western mode of discourse and provides a profound cultural alternative. According to the Talmud, man is commanded to study Torah. He fulfills this commandment when he makes an effort to understand and interpret not only his own guiding beliefs but the beliefs by which he chooses *not* to live. The writers of the Talmud understood the magnitude of the challenge. This is how they describe the perplexity of a man who studies Torah and suddenly meets the multitude of opinions within it: "Some of these Sages render an object or person ritually impure and these render it pure; these prohibit an action and these permit it; these deem an item invalid and these deem it valid. Lest a person say: Now, how can I study Torah when it contains so many different opinions?"[11]

The writers' answer is that the student must develop a special ability to listen, an "understanding heart" as they put it, to enable him to listen with empathy to any position and its opposite: "So too you, the student, make your ears like a funnel and acquire for yourself an understanding heart to hear both the statements of those who render objects ritually impure and the statements of those who render them pure; the statements of those who prohibit actions and the statements of those who permit them; the statements of those who deem items invalid and the statements of those who deem them valid."[12]

The Arab-Israeli conflict is not the only thing to hurt Israelis —their conversation about the conflict is hurting them as well. The conflict may deepen the rift between Israelis and their neighbors, but the way they talk about it deepens the rift between Israelis and other Israelis. In this section of the book I have touched on the conflict, but I have dealt mostly with Israelis' conversations *about* the conflict. I have sought throughout to acquire an understanding heart; to listen with empathy to different viewpoints; and, guided by the spirit of the Talmud, to try to rehabilitate Israel's fractured conversation.

PART III THE SPHERE OF PRAGMATIC DISCOURSE

Whenever a theory appears to you as the only possible one, take this as a sign that you have understood neither the theory nor the problem which it was intended to solve.

—Karl Popper

INTRODUCTION
The State and Its Dreams

For generations, the Jews dreamt a double dream: they dreamt of liberation from the rule of Gentiles and they dreamt of a life in the Land of Israel. The Zionist movement made both these dreams a reality. Israelis living in a free and sovereign Israel today do not always recognize that they represent a realization of these dreams. But the State of Israel did not just realize dreams—it also destroyed them. At the moment of its birth, Israel's founding father David Ben-Gurion made three painful ideological concessions: he sacrificed the state's secular character, he supported the partition of the land, and he compromised on the vision of socialism.

THE BLOW TO SECULARISM

For many Jews who arrived as part of the Second and Third Aliyot—the 1904–1914 and 1919–1923 waves of immigration—the transition was not just from Exile to the Land of Israel but from the strictures of religion to freedom from religion. They dreamt of a national life freed from the irrationality of tradition and liberated from the suffocating yoke of religious law. They placed David Ben-Gurion at the head of their political movement and tasked him with founding an enlightened, rational, and secular state. But Ben-Gurion failed to accomplish these goals. Instead, he forged an alliance with the ultra-Orthodox community, defining the relationship between religion and state in Israel and granting Orthodox rabbis control over the country's religious affairs. This produced a spectacular irony: the state created by secular rebels now enshrined religious legislation; the state conceived as a revolt against religion contained elements of religious coercion.

Why did Ben-Gurion do what he did? The answer can be found in the deliberations leading to the United Nations resolution of 29 November 1947, which proposed the partition of the land into two states, one Jewish and one Arab.[1] The United Nations reached its decision on the recommendations of a special committee sent to Palestine to examine whether the Jews and the Arabs could establish their own independent nation-states. This committee, known as UNSCOP, interviewed representatives of Palestine's Jewish population to determine whether this society could function as a sovereign state.

In the course of its fact-finding mission, UNSCOP also summoned representatives of the "Old Yishuv," the oldest Jewish community in the Land of Israel. Ben-Gurion was deeply concerned by this invitation. He was alarmed by the prospect that the ultra-Orthodox and mostly anti-Zionist members of the Old Yishuv might express their opposition to the establishment of a Jewish state, leading the committee to conclude that the Jews were not capable of establishing a stable state rooted in broad consensus across Jewish society. To counteract this threat, Ben-Gurion initiated an urgent dialogue with leaders of the Old Yishuv and brokered a fateful alliance: the ultra-Orthodox would agree not to undermine the diplomatic efforts to create a Jewish state and in exchange would receive influence over the Jewish character of that state. The fingerprints of this so-called status-quo agreement remain evident in the relationship between religion and state in Israel today. In order to enable the creation of the state, Ben-Gurion was willing to relinquish its secular character.

THE COMPROMISE OVER SOCIALISM

In the eyes of many of Israel's founders, the purpose of Zionism was to promote socialism. The future state, they believed, would liberate not only Jews from the rule of Gentiles but also workers from the rule of capitalists. The State of Israel would be both a safe haven for Jews and a society built on solidarity among workers. Ben-Gurion himself promoted this dual vision. As head of the Workers Party of the Land of Israel (the Mapai), he dreamt in the 1920s and 1930s of a classless and egalitarian society. But when he realized that these two visions could not be fully reconciled, Ben-Gurion opted for Zionism over socialism and pursued the interests of the state of the Jewish people over the status of the working class.

In the interests of *mamlachtiyut*—Ben-Gurion's overarching principle of prioritizing national interests over sectarian ones—Ben-Gurion disbanded the elite Palmach fighting units associated with the left. Likewise, he shut down the "Workers Stream"—the special education system for the working class—incorporating it into the national education system.[2]

But Ben-Gurion struck the most grievous blow to the socialist ethos when he opted for strategic relations with the United
States instead of the Soviet Union. The Communist Soviet Union
would have been a natural partner for a state founded by revolutionary immigrants from Russia who wanted to build a model socialist society in the Middle East. Ben-Gurion believed, however,
that the State of Israel would be stronger if it marched alongside
the capitalists of America. Despite the vigorous objections of his
comrades on the left, he chose to forge a strategic alliance with
the United States. Ben-Gurion judged that Israel's strength and
power were ultimately more important than the socialist vision
he was mandated to pursue.

THE PARTITION PLAN

When the idea of dividing the land between Jews and Arabs
first appeared on the Zionist movement's agenda at the end of
the 1930s, it was met with stiff resistance. One of its most force-
ful opponents was Menachem Ussishkin, who asked, "Is a nation
entitled to surrender its inheritance?" His answer was plain: "We
will not do that."[3] Ussishkin was speaking for many in the Zionist
movement: they feared that the demands of the various partition
plans that the Jews accept a shrunken state would ultimately
shrink their historical consciousness as well.

Ben-Gurion agreed with this assumption in principle, yet he
still backed partition. He adamantly believed that it was better to
relinquish the dream of sovereignty over the whole of the Land of
Israel in order to guarantee the creation of a state on a portion of
it. When the leaders of the Jewish Agency convened to debate the

U.N. Partition Plan, they accepted it with immense difficulty—five voted against and seven in favor. For Ben-Gurion, it was critical to stress that the vote was not the proposal of the Jewish Agency but rather a response to the proposal of the United Nations. He took great pains to clarify that the foundation of a Jewish state on only *part* of the land was not an aspiration of Zionism but a compromise by Zionists.

Ben-Gurion's visionary leadership transformed ideas into facts and dreams into reality, but in order to create these facts he had to abandon some of his dreams. He sacrificed the dream of secularism when he forged an alliance with the ultra-Orthodox; he compromised on socialism when he disbanded the Palmach, closed the workers' education system, and opted for an alliance with the United States; and he conceded on the unity of the land when he agreed to the U.N. Partition Plan. Had he not yielded ground to the ultra-Orthodox, the U.N. committee might not have recommended that a Jewish state be created. Had he not dissolved the institutions of socialism, the institutions of a nation-state could not have been built. Had he not compromised over the unity of the land, it would not have been possible to establish a state on even part of the land.

Conventional wisdom states that were it not for the great ideas and ideologies of Israel's founders, the State of Israel could not have been born. But in fact, the opposite is true: had Israel's founding fathers clung tenaciously to their ideologies, the state would never have been created at all. The state that was destined to fulfill so many dreams owes its very existence to the visionaries who were willing to relinquish those dreams.[4]

REPHRASING THE PROBLEM

Joseph Heller's famous novel *Catch-22,* published in 1961, centers on a narrative that unfolds during World War II. One of the book's heroes is Orr, a pilot who is driven crazy by constant aerial warfare. Soldiers who go insane are supposed to be discharged from military service, yet Orr cannot get released. Why? According to protocol, he needs to request a formal discharge. But if he is able to make such a request, this very act is taken as proof of his sanity, thereby undermining the grounds for his release.

That's the catch: in order to be declared unfit for fighting, a soldier must first plead insanity, but doing so inevitably proves the soldier's sanity and hence fitness to fight. The only action the pilot can take to release himself from military service is the same one that will ensure he cannot leave. This is the situation Heller calls "Catch-22." Over the years, the term has come to apply to any situation in which people find themselves trapped in an absurd impasse.

Israelis' thinking about the conflict with the Palestinians is mired in a similar "Catch-22" situation. They are trapped in an impossible no-win situation. The very action that can save them from the conflict is precisely the action that would deepen the conflict and make it worse. Withdrawing from the territories would transform the demographic problem into a security problem, whereas remaining in the territories would remove the security threat at the cost of perpetuating the demographic threat. The action that lifts one catastrophic peril merely converts it into another peril, no less catastrophic. This is Israel's "Catch-67."

Israelis' way of thinking would be so much more productive

if they stopped defining the situation as a "problem" and started framing it as a "catch" instead. Why? Because problems are meant to be solved—and this problem has no solution. A catch, however, is not meant to be solved—it is meant to be escaped from. And Israel's Catch-67 can almost certainly be escaped from too.

Searching for a way out of a catch rather than a solution to a problem creates lower and more realistic expectations than those behind grand diplomatic initiatives. Yet Israelis must not forget that even if they succeed in finding an escape route, the problem will not disappear; it will only change shape. It would be transformed from a problem that threatens Israel's existence into an essential part of Israel's existence.

The world of medicine deals with such problems: when an incurable disease attacks the human body, it can result in death. Some devastating diseases can be cured, while others do not allow for a complete recovery. Yet even when a fatal disease cannot be cured, those afflicted can still find ways to cope with it. Sometimes a medical intervention might not banish a malignant disease but can limit its damage. Such an intervention might turn a potentially fatal disease into a merely chronic one. Medicine teaches us that even when a threatening problem cannot be removed, hope exists that the threat can be removed from the problem.

For Israelis to escape the catch they must rescue themselves from the devastating choice between a state with a defensible Jewish majority but indefensible borders and a state with defensible borders but an endangered Jewish majority. They must forge a new reality in which the State of Israel has borders that allow it to defend itself from the Muslim majority surrounding it, without leaving it vulnerable to a potential Muslim majority within it. Various ideas have been raised for how to pave such an escape route from the catch, but every single one exacts a heavy price: to secure these escape routes and thereby Israel's continued existence, Israelis will have to relinquish some of Israel's dreams.

They will have to abandon dreams of a comprehensive peace agreement that will finally end the conflict, abolish the hostility directed against them, and provide Israel with internationally recognized borders. They will have to make their own peace with the fact that the drive to settle Judea and Samaria must come to an end, and that there will be no serious settlement construction in the historic, biblical heartland of the Jewish people. Coming to this dual realization—relinquishing both the sacred vision of peace and the sacred idea of settlement—can open up a broad intellectual landscape dotted with plans and ideas that have the potential to rescue the State of Israel from its present impossible predicament.

Israel's founders had to sacrifice some of their dreams so that the country could come into being. Now, Israelis too must sacrifice some of their dreams so that Israel may continue to exist. When they confront their Catch-67 and think about how they might save their country, they must return to Ben-Gurion's original pragmatism—the very force that created the country in the first place.

THIS BOOK IS NOT OVER

The book you are reading could have ended at the close of Part II. After exploring the major ideologies and examining their central arguments, I wrapped up with a philosophical take on Israel's political discourse. Indeed, my primary purpose in writing this book was not to offer a solution to Israel's political problems but to help heal Israel's political discourse. Yet if the book had ended there, it would have been incomplete. After proposing a practical, non-ideological approach as the key to rehabilitating Israeli discourse from its present malaise, I need also to clarify what such an approach would mean in practice. It is not enough merely to promote a pragmatic mode of thinking—it is essential to illustrate that mode as well. Indeed, as Jewish tradition teaches us, philosophy without practice is by its nature incomplete.

The work on the final, practical section of this book required me to break out of my comfort zone. Instead of reflecting on ideas, I set out to meet people. I conducted a series of discussions with figures in the Israeli security and intelligence establishments and in the Palestinian intellectual and cultural worlds. The people I met with asked to remain anonymous, but I thank them from the bottom of my heart for dozens of hours of engrossing conversation. Without them, I could never have rolled up my sleeves and moved from examining arguments to exploring practical policy.

I shall present two plans: the Partial-Peace Plan and the Divergence Plan. Some readers might be inclined to label the first as "moderate left" and the second as "moderate right," but I hope they will refrain from assigning labels. My aim is to distinguish not between left and right but between pragmatism and idealism. I believe both these plans illustrate how to make a transition toward a pragmatic mode of thinking.

The ideas I shall set out are not mine, nor are they new or original. Their components are drawn from the plans and ideas of experts, generals, and statesmen; I have collected them, polished them, and used them to construct two practical plans in different styles. Most important, I have arranged them inside the sphere of pragmatic discourse: a broad intellectual framework vast enough to encompass a wide and diverse range of practical ideas.

In laying out these proposals, I will not touch on such deep and complicated questions as the troubled status of Israeli Arabs, Israel's international image and reputation, or the relationship between the West Bank and the Gaza Strip, nor on other important problems that deserve profound and comprehensive consideration. I shall only present ideas that directly affect the catch at the center of this debate: a territorial withdrawal capable of saving Israel from one existential threat would inevitably create another.

The plans I describe here are presented as food for thought. Their purpose is not to persuade but to illustrate and mostly to encourage Israelis to lower their expectations. In doing so, they cannot hope to end the conflict and extinguish the hatred once and for all—but they can expect to transform a catastrophic problem into merely a chronic one, one that they can learn to live with.

10 THE PARTIAL-PEACE PLAN

Ever since the Six-Day War, the widespread conception among the Israeli defense establishment has been that Judea and Samaria are divided almost coincidentally into two zones: the areas most vital for Israel's defense are sparsely populated by Palestinians, while the areas most densely populated by Palestinians are those least critical for Israel's defense. This conception suggests a simple and elegant solution: Israel should relinquish the populated areas while retaining control over the areas it needs for its own defense. Thus, as if by magic, the occupation of the Palestinian people will end without endangering the Jewish people.

This basic idea, which comes in several different versions, is most identified with the plan proposed by Defense Minister Yigal Allon in July 1967.[1] The Allon Plan was based on the premise that a military presence in the Jordan Valley would render a withdrawal from the rest of the territories free of existential security dangers.[2] The underlying military logic is that an Israeli military presence in the Jordan Valley would guarantee the demilitarization of the state to be established to its west.[3] The area

Israel would evacuate, between the Jordan Valley to the east and the Green Line to the west, would be a non-Israeli zone, but its demilitarization would still be enforced by Israeli troops.[4] Under the Allon Plan, Israel would no longer extend from the Mediterranean Sea to the Jordan River, but its security border would remain the Jordan River.[5]

This plan was first put before the Israeli public immediately after the Six-Day War. The decades that have passed since then have not rendered it any less relevant. On the contrary, the security importance of the Jordan Valley has only increased since the events of the Arab Spring. The brutal chaos engulfing the Middle East, which has brought down regimes and obliterated prevailing orders, strengthens the argument that a continued Israeli military presence in the Jordan Valley remains absolutely critical in any future arrangement.

The collapse of the existing order in the Middle East has turned millions of people into refugees; many are fleeing from the region, but most are fleeing *within* the region. Many of these refugees are Palestinians.[6] If a Palestinian state were established, hundreds of thousands of these refugees would probably cross the Jordan River, flood Palestine, and destabilize a country that would only just have been established. The unplanned migration of millions of refugees into Palestine would transport with it the Middle East's chaos into Palestine's borders. Older and more established states have already succumbed to the forces of brutality unleashed by the Arab Spring. The transferal of these powerful forces into a new and vulnerable Palestine would probably provoke this new country's collapse.

The logic of an Israeli military presence in the Jordan Valley has rested until now on the case that it would prevent the entry of military forces or the smuggling of masses of weapons into Palestine.[7] To this we must sadly add that an Israeli military presence would prevent the migration of masses of people into Palestine as well. Israel's military presence in the Jordan Valley, therefore, would have two purposes: it would prevent the militarization of a Palestinian state, but it would also prevent its collapse.[8] In this argument, Israel's military presence in the Jordan Valley would enable it to defend itself from the threat of Palestine as well as from the threat of Palestine's collapse. If both these distinctions are reasonable, then the conclusion that follows is also reasonable: an Israeli military presence in the Jordan Valley is an effective defensive barrier, protecting Israel from a raging Middle East and enabling it to withdraw from the rest of the territories without gambling on its own continued survival.[9]

INTERNALIZING THE PRAGMATIC SHIFT

If the Allon Plan is so elegant and simple, why has it never been pursued? The reason is that not a single statesman in the whole Arab world would ever agree to it. Even if a Palestinian leader were daring enough to urge his people to accept a historic compromise, conceding the right of return, such a leader could only do so for a state encompassing the entire West Bank, not just a part of it. The hypothetical scenario in which a Palestinian leader might be prepared to relinquish the return of both refugees and territory is unrealistic in the extreme. The Allon Plan in its various guises was a plan on which Israelis could agree among themselves, but it was never a plan to which the Palestinians could agree as well. Over the years, when it became clear that the Allon Plan could not form the basis for a peace agreement, it receded from the public debate and disappeared.

The Allon Plan's great weakness was that it purported to solve the conflict.[10] But what if Israelis abandoned this pretension? What if instead of asking whether the plan could *solve* the conflict, they asked instead whether it could rescue Israel from the trap—from the Catch-67? If Israelis internalized the need for pragmatic thinking and looked for a lifeline *from* the conflict instead of a solution *to* it, then this plan, with certain adjustments, would deserve to be examined anew.

The Camp David Accords between Israel and Egypt set a precedent whereby the Arab side would agree to sign a full peace treaty only after a complete and total withdrawal from the territories by Israel. This formula formed the basis of future discussions about diplomatic solutions: peace would only be as extensive as Israel's withdrawal. The traditional understanding of this formula is that in exchange for a comprehensive peace accord, Israel would have to execute a comprehensive withdrawal. But perhaps it would be wiser to understand the equation differently: Israel could execute a partial withdrawal in exchange for a partial peace accord.

Such an arrangement would require the Palestinians neither to relinquish their demand to resettle the refugees nor to recognize Israeli sovereignty over holy Muslim soil as permanent— nor would it require Israel to withdraw from all of the conquered territories. Israel would remain in control of the settlement blocs and certain security zones. This would not be a deal to forge peace but to terminate a state of war.

It is easy to forget, but precedents exist not only for a peace treaty based on a full withdrawal but also for a partial agreement based on a partial withdrawal. Such was the agreement that Israel, under Prime Minister Yitzhak Rabin, signed with Egypt in 1975 through the mediation of Henry Kissinger. Israel agreed to withdraw its forces dozens of miles from the ceasefire lines, also conceding lucrative oil fields, but kept its forces stationed in other parts of the Sinai Peninsula. The Sinai Interim Agreement was not intended to forge peace but to terminate a state of war. This accord was never imprinted on the public's consciousness because it was followed three years later by the sensational and dramatic Camp David Accords, which left the interim agreements of Rabin and Kissinger in the shade.

The aspiration to repeat a comprehensive peace treaty with the Palestinians, similar to the follow-up accord with Egypt, has been obstructing political progress for decades. It would seem that the precedent with the best chance of repetition is not the follow-up peace treaty with Egypt but its predecessor, the interim accord. This means pursuing the legacy of Rabin over that of Begin, and seeking to repeat the more moderate deal brokered by Kissinger over the sweeping peace deal brokered at Camp David. A partial withdrawal for a partial peace.

In conclusion: if the Jordan Valley and the settlement blocs remained in Israeli hands, then the Palestinian state that would arise on the remainder of the West Bank would have territorial contiguity without shrinking Israel to indefensible proportions.[11] A partial withdrawal, then, would extract Israel from its present trap. It would abolish Israel's direct military rule over Palestinian civilians on the one hand while keeping Israel militarily defended on the other.

A partial agreement would also save the Palestinians from a trap no less constricting.

THE PALESTINIAN TRAP

The Israeli public conceives of a permanent agreement that would end the conflict—the object of diplomatic efforts for decades —as a straightforward exchange of land for peace. But this is the wrong way to characterize such a trade-off. A better description would be this: 1967 for 1948. Such a peace agreement would require the Palestinians to relinquish the right of return and Israel to relinquish land. Israel would pull back from the territories it captured in 1967, and the Palestinians would agree to forgo the return of the 1948 refugees to Israel. Land for refugees.

The problem with such an exchange is that in the Palestinian narrative the trauma of 1948 is greater than that of 1967. The memories of the tragedy of 1948 haunt the Palestinians more than the occupation of 1967. If, in exchange for Israel's relinquishing the territories, the Palestinians are asked to relinquish the right of return, this means that in exchange for a state, they are being asked to turn their backs on five million refugees. The agreement under discussion is a demand that the Palestinians betray their own nation in order to make peace with another nation—with the Israelis.[12]

This is not only a question of national betrayal: for many Palestinians, it would also be a religious offense. In the common understanding, there can be no religious legitimacy for non-Islamic sovereignty over territory that once belonged to Islam. The Land of Israel was under Islamic rule for centuries, and this is why Palestinians consider Jewish sovereignty religiously illegitimate and why Muslims are commanded to wage war to abolish that sovereignty.[13] Israel's demand that the Palestinians declare an end to the conflict and renounce all their claims is a demand that they recognize alien sovereignty over Islamic lands as permanent and eternal. Any Palestinian state based on a comprehensive peace agreement with Israel would be a state founded at the expense of Islamic law.[14]

For Palestinians to agree to terminate the conflict and renounce their claims would therefore be a betrayal of the refugees and an offense against religious law. To make peace, the Palestinians would have to commit a sin against their own faith and against their own people.[15]

The Israelis are, thus, not the only people caught in a trap—so are the Palestinians. This is the Palestinians' trap: their only route to a sovereign and independent state runs through a transformation of their religious and national identity. The preservation of their national and religious loyalties will continue to deprive them of independent statehood. A framework along the lines of Ehud Barak's offer, the Clinton Parameters, or the Olmert proposal would leave the Palestinians in a catch of their own. It is hardly surprising that when the Palestinians are pushed into a corner and compelled to choose between their identity and their independence, the majority opt for their identity.

But an alternative exists. Islamic jurisprudence permits the signing of a ceasefire agreement with the enemy on condition that it not be permanent. In Islamic tradition such a temporary ceasefire agreement, which does not require Muslims to recognize the legitimacy of the other side, is termed a *hudna*. As opposed to a deal asking the Palestinians to betray their religion, a hudna would be part of their religion.[16] It must be stressed that a partial-peace agreement is not the same as an interim agreement. It is not a preliminary stage laying the groundwork for a permanent accord: for the Palestinians, any permanent accord would require them to conclusively relinquish the dream of returning the refugees and to recognize the permanence of alien sovereignty over Islamic land. This is why the hudna would have to be devoid of any rhetoric suggesting it applied for eternity, and divorced from any indication of permanence. Paradoxically, the more an accord was understood as partial and temporary, the more stable and secure it would be.

Herein lies one of the greatest advantages of the Partial-Peace Plan: it liberates Israelis and Palestinians alike from their respective traps. In exchange for a long-term ceasefire agreement with Israel, the Palestinians would receive a sovereign state with territorial contiguity, without having to recognize Israel and without renouncing the right of return.[17]

To conclude: Israel's partial withdrawal from the territories, without the Palestinians' commitment to end all their claims, would rescue Israel and the Palestinians from their respective traps. The Israelis would be released from the occupation without endangering their security, and the Palestinians would receive a state without altering their fundamental identity.

A NEW MIDDLE EAST

For years, the great diplomatic aspiration of the international community has been to forge an agreement between Israel and the Palestinians that would terminate the conflict and end the claims of both sides against each other. But every diplomatic attempt to solve the conflict has hit a dead end. The way out, some argue, is for the Israelis to make even grander offers than they have in the past, in order to tempt the Palestinians to sign a peace agreement.

The political logic of the Partial-Peace Plan is the reverse of this thinking. Instead of Israel offering the Palestinians more, it should expect from them less. In a partial accord, the Palestinians would be expected neither to forgo the return of refugees, nor to reconcile themselves to alien sovereignty over Islamic soil, nor even to agree to end the conflict permanently or renounce all their claims. The formula is simple enough: the Palestinians would not compromise their basic identity, and Israelis would not compromise their security. One of the twentieth century's greatest diplomats, Henry Kissinger, understood long ago that when a complete diplomatic solution is impossible, a partial solution is the way forward.[18]

Such an argument sounds rational, simple, and desirable, but reality is more complicated. The Palestinian intellectuals I interviewed for this book assessed the chances of the Palestinians agreeing to a partial agreement as low. The aftermath of the Oslo Accords taught the Palestinians to be highly suspicious of interim agreements, and they could interpret a partial accord as such. They fear that these are cunning attempts by the stronger party to perpetuate the occupation and their humiliation. That said, current changes taking place across the Middle East might engender a friendlier political climate toward the idea of a partial agreement.

The Middle East is undergoing a transformation. The political earthquake of recent years has diverted international attention toward two crises that dwarf the Arab-Israeli conflict: the clash between Arab nation-states and the Islamic State, and the historical confrontation between the Shiite and Sunni factions. These upheavals are shaking up the regional order and undermining old certainties, but they also present Israel with a political opportunity. Several Arab states now have an interest in establishing a Sunni-Israeli axis as a counterweight to the Shia axis. The Sunni states no longer view the Palestinian question as the main issue on their agenda, and it appears that they want to find a way to banish it to the sidelines, even if it cannot be solved.

The Arab states are also in a catch: the accepted approach of making the end of Israel's control of the territories a condition for the resolution of the refugee problem has perpetuated Israel's control of the territories, thereby hindering attempts to establish normal and healthy relations between the Arab world and Israel. The end of military rule over the population in the territories is in Israel's interests—but it is also in the Saudis' interests, in Egypt's interests, and in the other Gulf states' interests.

The Sunni Arab states can help to create a climate in which the Palestinians will feel comfortable with a partial solution—a deal that ends Israel's control of most of the territories east of the Green Line without recognizing the legitimacy of Jewish sovereignty in the territories west of the Green Line.[19]

THE CONFLICT WILL ENDURE

Even after a peace accord is signed and a ceasefire declared, we can reasonably assume that the conflict will endure. We can assume that the deal will be violated at some point, and the violence resumed. The historical forces perpetuating this conflict are too stubborn, the sectarian identities fueling it too mighty. A non-belligerency pact is unlikely to end the fighting in the long run.

But if the parties turn their energies toward pragmatic thinking, they will be able to think differently about the purpose of political initiatives. The power of a partial agreement is not that it ends the conflict but that it restructures it. The new borders sketched by such an agreement would not abolish the conflict but rather transform its character. They would convert it from a conflict between a state and its subjects into a conflict between a state and its neighbors. As such, this initiative would not give Israel complete security, but it would give it *existential* security. This process would not remove the threat to the lives of Israelis, but it would remove the threat to the life of Israel itself.

This is not a matter of "managing the conflict." That euphemism is synonymous nowadays with perpetuating the status quo. The purpose of restructuring the conflict, in contrast, is to change it from the bottom up. The Partial-Peace Plan converts a conflict between occupier and occupied at home into a conflict between a state and its enemies abroad. It is vital to restructure the conflict in order to continue dealing with it. In contrast to the prevailing paradigm, in which new borders must be delineated in order to bring peace, in this plan new borders must be delineated in order to better manage a state of war, as and when it resumes.

The desire for a permanent accord has been frustrated time and time again over the years, floundering in confrontation with the most explosive issues of the conflict, chiefly the fate of the refugees and the final status of Jerusalem. The abandonment of the demand for an end to the conflict and an end to all claims is precisely what saves the Partial-Peace Plan from dealing with these thorny questions. Final borders, the future of Jerusalem, the question of refugees, West Bank–Gaza relations, and countless other core issues would not even be on the table in negotiations for the Partial-Peace Plan.[20] Every one of these issues would continue to bedevil Israeli-Palestinian relations even after the signing of a partial accord. But it is precisely the partial and defective nature of this plan that makes it easiest for Israeli society to accept. The Partial-Peace Plan would minimize the occupation and guarantee Israel's existential security, thereby addressing the principal fears of both the new left and the new right. That is why it enjoys the potential for widespread consensus across Israeli society.

11 THE DIVERGENCE PLAN

Israeli pragmatists are those Israelis whose opinions are not part of their identity. Politics is not the sphere in which they express their tribal belonging but the arena in which they confront the challenges that threaten their existence. The Partial-Peace Plan illustrates the pragmatists' way of thinking, but it represents a rather dramatic example of such thinking because it aims to redraw the state's borders. It would behoove us, therefore, to explore more modest proposals that would not leave Jewish settlements outside the zone of Israeli control.

One such intriguing direction was proposed by Henry Kissinger. In late 2016, the senior statesman expressed doubt about the possibility of establishing an independent Palestinian state in the present day and age. In an interview for the *Atlantic* magazine, Kissinger observed that powerful forces are smashing existing nation-states across the Middle East. Libya has collapsed, as have Iraq and Syria. Under present conditions, a new, tiny Palestine would not survive. But according to Kissinger, the political alternative to an independent and sovereign Palestinian state is not the perpetuation of the status quo but amplification and meaningful empowerment of certain elements that already exist. Israel, Kissinger says, must enlarge the Palestinian Authority's powers, zones of control, national symbols, and attributes of sovereignty, thereby expanding its autonomy until it functions almost like a state—but none of this would require the Palestinians to regard the result as an end of the conflict or to agree to renounce all further claims.[1]

Another interesting direction was proposed by A. B. Yehoshua. In late 2016, the celebrated Israeli author announced that he had concluded that the creation of a fully independent Palestinian state was impossible for the foreseeable future. Like Kissinger, Yehoshua also believes that whereas a comprehensive deal is unattainable, partial steps to minimize the occupation are possible. Yehoshua proposed an initiative to ameliorate the situation of all the Palestinians who do not live under Palestinian autonomy. In his view, the more than fifty thousand (and perhaps as many as three hundred thousand) Palestinians who live in Area C of the West Bank should be allowed to become residents of the State of Israel.[2]

Kissinger proposes bolstering Palestinian autonomy; Yehoshua proposes bolstering the rights of the Palestinians who do not live under self-rule. The common thread between these two ideas can serve as inspiration for a pragmatic initiative to rescue Israel from its Catch-67. In what follows, I shall sketch the outlines of one such possible pragmatic initiative as food for thought.

THE ALMOST STATE

The first plank of the Divergence Plan, the Kissingerian one, could be implemented by combining two efforts—diplomatic and territorial. The purpose of the diplomatic effort would be to boost the symbolic potency of the Palestinian entity, and the purpose of the territorial effort would be to increase the extent of the Palestinians' day-to-day and practical freedom. Together, these efforts would offer Palestinians greater separation from Israel with less security risk to Israelis.[3]

The Diplomatic Effort

The Palestinian Authority sees itself as a political entity separate and independent from Israel. This attitude is a positive asset for Israel. Some experts fear that such an attitude cannot be taken for granted, and that Israel must actively nurture and amplify it. Of all the actions that could contribute to the symbolic empowerment of Palestinian independence, two could be particularly effective. The first would be Israel's recognition of the Palestinian Authority as the State of Palestine.

The Palestinian Authority has been waging a diplomatic offensive in recent years for international recognition of its independence. The pinnacle of its aspirations is to persuade the United Nations General Assembly and Security Council to recognize a State of Palestine as a full and independent member of the family of nations. Israel, meanwhile, is attempting to combat this effort for international recognition. It has succeeded in enlisting the diplomatic might of the United States to prevent the recognition of the State of Palestine in the Security Council. The argument that Israel and the United States make is based on conventional political logic, that the goal of the Middle East peace process is to achieve peace between Israel and the Palestinians, such that the establishment of a Palestinian state should only come within the framework of a permanent accord with Israel.

If Israelis opt to change their way of thinking, however, and replace their hope for peace with hope for an escape from their present trap, then Israel's attitude toward international recognition of Palestine should change accordingly. As long as Israel holds out hope of solving the conflict, an international recognition of Palestine before the successful conclusion of negotiations would indeed be problematic. But if Israel chose instead to settle for restructuring the conflict, then international recognition of Palestine could be an advantage.[4] That is to say, Israel should stop fighting the Palestinian Authority's diplomatic offensive and join it instead.[5]

Israel could also explore an additional policy, which would dramatically enhance the Palestinian entity's symbolic capital: a physical capital in East Jerusalem. Israel could transfer certain East Jerusalem neighborhoods to the control of the Palestinian polity. Several East Jerusalem neighborhoods contain neither Jewish history nor Jewish residents; their transfer to Palestinian hands would not undermine Israel's symbolic capital but would vastly enhance Palestine's. Not only would the Palestinian Authority become a recognized state, it would also have a recognized capital—in Jerusalem.[6]

The Territorial Effort

The chief obstacle to Palestinian independence is not symbolic but practical. Movement across the West Bank is controlled by the Israeli military. Even though most of the Arabs of the West Bank live under Palestinian Authority (P.A.) control, if they want to travel from one P.A.-controlled area to another they are almost invariably required to cross territory under Israel's full control—Area C. In other words, while their place of residence is under their (relative) control, their movement is not. The Palestinians' sense of occupation comes mostly from travel through Area C, where they have to pass checkpoints, are stopped by occasional patrols, and find themselves in daily friction with Israeli soldiers.

Israel can set itself a strategic objective to abolish all these points of friction and to boost the Palestinians' practical freedom. This would require Israel to enlarge the territories under Palestinian control by handing over sections of Area C to the Palestinian Authority and pursuing a range of technological and infrastructural means—including bridges, tunnels, and bypasses—to enable Palestinians living in P.A. areas to move freely from point to point without passing through areas under Israeli control.[7] This would be a major and complex architectural undertaking, but it is a strategic project that Israel has the ability to take on. Even if it were not possible to achieve territorial contiguity between all the areas under enhanced Palestinian autonomy, it could still be possible to achieve transportation contiguity between them. Additionally, Israel would prevent the expansion of settlements outside the main blocs so as not to create new security constraints that might impede Palestinian transportation contiguity.

The combination of these two efforts, the diplomatic and the territorial, would bolster the impression of Palestinian sovereignty in symbolic terms and minimize the control over the Palestinians in practical terms.[8] These efforts would merge to create a meaningful process of separation.[9]

The Divergence Plan is not a solution to the conflict but an illustration of how it might be restructured: on the one hand, Israel would neither evacuate settlements nor vacate its army; but on the other, Palestinian self-rule would extend over a territory whose areas were all linked with transportation contiguity—and with a capital in Jerusalem.[10]

ALMOST CITIZENS

Although most of the Palestinians in the West Bank reside in Areas A and B, tens if not hundreds of thousands live outside the areas of Palestinian self-rule. The Palestinians of Area C are an Arab population that has fallen between the cracks. They enjoy neither Israeli citizenship like the Arabs who live in Israel nor self-rule like the Arabs living under the Palestinian Authority. They are governed directly by the Israeli military, their movement is restricted, and their rights are continuously violated.

The problem facing the Palestinians of Area C is severe for yet another reason. Area C is also where the Jewish settlers live, creating an environment in which Jews who are citizens of Israel and Palestinians who are occupied by Israel live side by side. The difference between these two populations creates an exceptionally painful and unpleasant situation of discrimination. The policies outlined above would enhance Palestinian self-rule, but they would do nothing for the Palestinians who find themselves living outside P.A. territory. In addition to increasing Palestinian autonomy and enlarging its territory, therefore, Israel must pursue a complementary process to address the needs of the residents of areas beyond the realm of Palestinian self-rule.

Israel could permit tens of thousands of Palestinians in Area

C to become residents of the State of Israel. In such a situation, the Palestinians of Area C would enjoy the same rights awarded to the Arabs of East Jerusalem. As A. B. Yehoshua argued, "By upgrading their status, and giving them national insurance and unemployment benefits, you would reduce the toxicity of the occupation in Area C."[11] This is not a case of annexing the territory but granting rights to the people who inhabit it.[12] Such a policy would exact a price, but Israel's overwhelming Jewish majority would not be undermined by the addition of a few tens of thousands of new residents. This action would create a new reality, in which the gap between the settlers and the Palestinians who dwell among them would shrink drastically, the existing discrimination would be abolished, and the violated rights of the Palestinians would be restored.

In short: the Divergence Plan is based on two parallel, complementary processes. The first is the expansion of the zone of Palestinian self-rule, the enhancement of its powers, and the infrastructural connection of its various areas; and the second is the extension of Israeli residency rights to the Palestinians who live outside of the areas of Palestinian self-rule. On the one hand, Areas A and B would be expanded and would almost be a state; on the other, the remaining residents of Area C would almost be citizens of the Israeli state. The result would be a dramatic contraction of Israel's control over the Palestinians, without a dramatic contraction of Israel's security.

12 POLITICAL PRAGMATISM AS A BRIDGE BETWEEN THE LEFT AND THE RIGHT

TWO RESPONSES TO CATCH-67

What I offer in this book is a new Israeli package deal, to abandon two great dreams in order to meet two basic needs. Israelis would abandon the dream of a diplomatic accord to bring peace and the dream of a settlement project to bring redemption, but would be guaranteed a state that is both Jewish and well defended.[1] Both plans presented here represent an attempt to create such a package deal. That said, these plans are still radically different, containing many variations between them. It is tempting to categorize the Partial-Peace Plan as "moderate left" and the Divergence Plan as "moderate right." But such a temptation is rooted in the bad habits of long-held thinking patterns, which I hope Israelis will be able to kick.

One difference between the two plans is qualitative: the Partial-Peace Plan is based on an external act of political intervention to remake the current situation while the Divergence

Plan is based on the amplification and enhancement of conditions inherent in the current situation. A further difference is quantitative: the Partial-Peace Plan would minimize the occupation more than the Divergence Plan, but the Divergence Plan would entail fewer security risks than the Partial-Peace alternative.[2] Despite these differences, both initiatives rely on the same principles. Neither initiative aims to solve the problem—only to extract Israel from the trap of the Catch-67. Neither hopes to solve the conflict, only to convert it from a fatal situation into a chronic one.

In the course of writing this book, I pitched these two initiatives to various audiences in order to gauge their reactions. The responses necessarily varied, but one response was repeated among almost every group: "But this doesn't solve the conflict." Skeptics on the right protested that the plans would not eliminate the security threats, and skeptics on the left were angry that the plans kept the IDF in part of the territories.

The responses left me both surprised and frustrated. "Did they not hear what I just said?" I asked myself. After all, I had repeatedly emphasized that these initiatives did not purport to achieve total security, but only to offer existential security; I had repeatedly stressed that they did not claim to solve the conflict, only to extricate Israel from the trap. This persistent response taught me just how powerful Israelis' habits of thought truly are. On everything to do with the Arab-Israeli conflict, their habits of thought are preventing them from progressing beyond thinking in dichotomies to thinking in degrees.

Ideological thinking about this issue tends to be dichotomous: either Israel is an occupying power or it is a moral society;

either Israel is at war or it is at peace; either Israel is settling the land or it is betraying its own identity and values. A pragmatic mode of thinking, however, would see the situation in terms of degrees. The former New York City mayor Rudy Giuliani is often credited with the dramatic reduction in the city's crime rate. No one argues that Giuliani failed on crime simply because people are still murdered on the city's streets. Similarly, any leader who manages to dramatically reduce the number of deaths from traffic accidents is considered to have been successful even if people are still killed in accidents on the nation's roads.

When it comes to traffic accidents and crime, people think in degrees—but when it comes to the Israeli-Palestinian conflict, Israelis have become accustomed to thinking in dichotomies. They never ask how to reduce the incidence of terrorism; they want to know how to eliminate it. They never ask how to reduce the intensity of the conflict, only how to solve it. They never ask how to minimize the occupation, only how to end it.

THE TWO PLANS AS FOOD FOR THOUGHT

As I have already written, the territories are not occupied but the Palestinians are a people under occupation. Whoever accepts this distinction can also accept the conclusion that follows: the more that Israel reduces the extent of its control over the Palestinians, the more it will minimize the occupation of the Palestinians. Israel's withdrawal from populated Palestinian areas, the removal of restrictions on Palestinian identity, and free movement for Palestinians on the West Bank would constitute a meaningful reduction of Israel's control over the Palestinians, even if Israel remained on a portion of the disputed territory. In other words, these pragmatic initiatives would not only release Israel from its existential catch, they would also minimize the current moral problem.

The international community does not and probably would not accept the distinction between the occupation of land and the occupation of people, so initiatives of this sort would neither relieve international pressure nor heal Israel's complicated relations with the capitals of Europe. But since these initiatives would seriously reduce the friction between Israelis and Palestinian civilians, they would also seriously reduce the friction between Israel and the international community. More important, they would probably contribute to healing the relations between Israelis and many young Jews across the Diaspora. Since these plans would reduce the moral problem inherent in imposing military rule over a civilian population, they would remove some of the emotional barriers that separate Jewish youth in the Diaspora from Israel.

No one who imposes a binary way of thinking on the conflict can be expected to become reconciled to initiatives of this sort. These plans do not offer complete security for the citizens of Israel; they proffer only existential security for the State of Israel. They do not end the occupation of land; they only minimize control over people. No one who expects political initiatives to cure all the ills plaguing the situation and to guarantee lasting peace, total security, and pure morality will feel comfortable with the compromises proposed in this book. Conversely, whoever takes up the challenge and starts thinking in degrees is likely to find in these pragmatic initiatives much fruitful food for thought.

THE PRAGMATIC SPHERE AND THE REHABILITATION OF THE ISRAELI CONVERSATION

A new politics that bridges the gulf between the left and the right could emerge from an intellectual sphere defined by pragmatism. Such an intellectual sphere would be based on three new answers to three old questions:

Q: What is expected from changing the State of Israel's eastern border?

A: The purpose of amending borders is not to end the conflict but to restructure it.

Q: What is expected from a political initiative?

A: The purpose of a political initiative is not to solve a problem but to convert it from an existential problem to one that is containable.

Q: What is the role of political dreams?

A: Israelis should embrace a great package deal: the abandonment of sacred dreams in exchange for the acquisition of existential needs.

Israel's ideological crises caused many on the right to give up on the people because the people had given up on the Land of Israel, and caused many on the left to give up on the people because the people had given up on peace. But these processes occurred at the margins: the great majority of Israelis did not give up; they adapted. The right exchanged redemption for security as its primary concern, and the left exchanged peace for the occupation as its primary concern. The old left and old right were destined to collide, but the new right and the new left are able to talk instead—because while peace and redemption come at the expense of one another, security and the end of the occupation can come *hand in hand*. In other words, Israel's present crisis of ideas grants it its greatest opportunity for genuine dialogue.

WAR AND PEACE

The Partial-Peace Plan, the Divergence Plan, and other pragmatic initiatives illustrate a modest conception of politics, which is about not solving problems but restructuring them. Such humility pertains to what might be expected from peace as well as to what might be expected from war. Few people realize that moving on from believing in the possibility of peace is the mirror image of moving on from believing in the possibility of victory in war. For decades, wars have not ended with victories. In a world of asymmetric warfare, there is no such thing as victory. American power did not win in Vietnam; Soviet power did not win in Afghanistan; Israeli power did not win in Lebanon; and the IDF has been unable to score a decisive victory in repeated rounds of war in Gaza. In every war, the people demand victory—and emerge embittered when confronted with equivocal and ambiguous results.

Just as there can be no victory in war, neither can there be victory in peace. Just as the military cannot win decisively, neither can politicians and diplomats. Peace agreements are achieved between strong and stable states; military victories are achieved between organized, regular armies. The disintegration of countries into small tribal clusters and fragmented terrorist groups has produced a reality of wars that cannot be won and peace agreements that cannot be trusted.

The right's rallying cry, "Let the IDF Win!" is equally as absurd as the left's demand, "Peace Now." The left reminds Israelis repeatedly that they cannot win the war, and the right reminds them repeatedly that they cannot win the peace—and they are both correct! But they are also both wrong. The modern world calls on Israelis to lower their expectations of both war and peace, and to move from a politics that attempts to change reality toward a politics that finds a way to live with it instead.

AFTERWORD

The founder of Political Zionism, Theodor Herzl, opposed the attempt to revive the Hebrew tongue. He believed that Hebrew was dead and could never be resurrected. Herzl's skepticism was well grounded, because there was no precedent for taking a disused, ancient language and reviving it as the spoken tongue of a living, breathing nation.

The founder of Cultural Zionism, Ahad Ha'am, opposed the plan to gather the majority of the Jewish people in the Land of Israel. He believed that the land was a wilderness and could never absorb a critical mass of the Jewish people. His skepticism was also well grounded, because there was no precedent for taking a nation dispersed across the globe and gathering it anew in its ancient homeland.

For their times, both Theodor Herzl and Ahad Ha'am were right. Rationally speaking, the revival of the Hebrew tongue and the ingathering of the exiles were impossible tasks—but in hindsight, we know that they were wrong. The Zionist movement was able to triumph over the pessimism of its founders.

The pioneers of the Hebrew language revival devoted themselves to the impossible task of resurrecting a dead language; the pioneers of the workers' settlement movement devoted themselves to the impossible task of making the desert bloom and absorbing waves of immigrants; the pioneers of the early Hebrew defense forces devoted themselves to the impossible task of establishing a new state and defending it. The complete self-sacrifice of the assorted pioneers rendered the impossible possible. The great majority believed in redemptive ideologies. We can assume that without their conviction in these total ideologies, they would never have been able to muster the total self-sacrifice necessary to change the course of Jewish history.[1]

In this book I offer an indictment of total ideologies, but the truth is that without such redemptive ideologies, the Zionist project would never have been able to surmount its many obstacles and establish itself against all odds.

In *Catch-67* I have sought to expose the ideological fixations created by such unequivocal beliefs, and to argue that escaping the catch requires leaving these ideological fixations behind. Revolutionary ideologies were indeed necessary to bring Zionism into existence, but their softening and maturation are equally necessary for Zionism to survive and to prosper.

UNCOMPROMISING MORALITY

Ideological compromises are forged in the sober encounter between ideology and reality, but an ideological compromise is not necessarily a *moral* compromise. On the contrary, I believe that a position of pragmatism would be a position of uncompromising morality. How so? I shall try to illustrate this through the final speech of none other than Moses.

When the Israelites were in Egypt, they were threatened by

the power of Egypt; but when they entered the Promised Land, they were threatened by their own power, which threatened to corrupt their very character. In his final speech to the nation, Moses described the fear of the power of others as a fear of returning to Egypt—but he described the fear of the corrupting nature of one's own power as a fear of turning *into* Egypt. The Bible does not ask us to banish these fears. Instead, it demands that we learn to live with them both. These two biblical fears continue to challenge life in Israel today, because the State of Israel is extremely strong—but at the same time it is also extremely weak.

Israel is extremely strong. Born in the mid-twentieth century, it won a string of military victories and soared in a short time from a third-world economy to an advanced and prosperous Western economy. Israel's gross domestic product per capita of $37,200 is larger than that of all its neighbors—Egypt, Jordan, Syria, and Lebanon—combined.[2] Israel has produced more start-ups per capita than any country in Europe. Tiny Israel is one of the few countries in the world with satellites in space and, according to foreign media, nuclear capabilities.

But many Israelis fear that Israel is also extremely fragile. It is located at the heart of the chaos sweeping the Middle East, surrounded both by barbaric and unpredictable terror organizations that hate it and by large, strong states that want to destroy it. Some of these states and organizations are also developing their ability to do so. Furthermore, forces that seek to isolate Israel are on the rise in Europe. This combination of a fear of isolation together with a fear of violence creates a mentality of weakness. Many Israelis feel, with justification, that despite achieving sovereignty, they remain a minority: no longer a minority *within* a country but a minority *as* a country.

Since Israel is so fragile, anyone who warns of the threat posed by outside powers is absolutely right. And since Israel is so strong, anyone who warns of the threat posed by the corrupting effect of the country's own power is equally right. The problem is that the same people rarely ring the same alarm bells. Most of my close friends in Israel who are hypersensitive to the dangers of a hostile Middle East tend to be apathetic about the human rights of the Palestinians. Most of my close friends who are hypersensitive about the rights of the Palestinians tend to be apathetic about the great danger that surrounds them from the outside.

Each camp has taken exclusive ownership of a single fear. One camp is afraid of returning to Egypt, and the other camp is afraid of turning into Egypt. In Jewish tradition, the Israelites entering the Promised Land were posed a challenge: to balance these fears. In the spirit of this biblical tradition, a shift toward pragmatic politics would offer a way to smash both the left's monopoly on the fear of the corrupting potential of Israel's power and the right's monopoly on the fear of the threatening power of Israel's enemies—and to nurture a Zionism that is able to confront both their fears simultaneously.

Pragmatism is not a style of politics devoid of moral conviction. On the contrary, pragmatism is based on a complex moral conviction, one that is totally uncompromising. It is one that refuses to renounce either moral concern but rather insists on clinging to both of them without compromise.

Neither to return to Egypt, nor to turn into Egypt.

THE QUEST FOR MEANING

Human beings search for meaning, which is why they search for belonging. Belonging to a community, a movement, or an idea that is larger than the individual imbues life with meaning. The great political ideologies filled with meaning the lives of the many Israelis who devoted themselves to them. The faith that Jewish history was marching inexorably toward Middle East peace gave birth to the Israeli peace movement. The belief that settlement construction on the ancient biblical soil of Judea and Samaria would expedite the Redemption gave birth to the Israeli settlement movement. This, too, is a belief loaded with emotion, and it filled the lives of its adherents with meaning.

Herein lies the primary difference between ideological and pragmatic politics: ideological politics deals with meaning; pragmatic politics deals mostly with survival. This is also the weakness of pragmatic politics. What sense of meaning can we possibly retain if we have to give up the great ideas that first filled our lives with the adrenaline of idealism? If the political sphere is but a cold and rational space in which to evaluate ideas on their efficiency, rather than one in which to express belonging, then its citizens might be blessed with realism—but are they not also left alienated and isolated?

This profound quandary has, for Israelis, an ancient answer: choosing a political sphere devoid of ideologies does not entail an absence of belonging because the foundations of a new Israeli pragmatism are not shallow—rather, they are rooted deep in the ancient Jewish tradition.

The Hebrew Bible was revolutionary. The world in which it was written and in which the prophets roamed was a world that worshipped political power. The Egyptians and Mesopotamians believed that kings were gods and that monarchy was part of the religious order. The pagan world did not just obey its kings—it worshipped them. This was the world the Bible set out to challenge.

The Bible operates against the myth that those who hold political power also hold the status of gods. In a daring literary escapade, the Bible exposes the weaknesses and deficiencies of David and Solomon and thereby proclaims their unmistakable humanity. The Bible systematically denies the divine nature of kings and the eternality of the political order. The heroes of the Bible, the prophets, were not the holders of political power but its most vigorous critics. Compared to the ancient pagan world, the biblical faith was heresy. Heresy against the sanctity of politics.

In the modern era, Europe gave rise to great political ideologies, all based on a faith in the redemptive power of ideas. Some people blindly followed socialism, others placed their faith in fascism, and others believed unreflectively in liberalism. They all believed that their respective ideologies were perfect, and that if only those ideologies could be implemented, the world would be perfect as well. If the ancient world worshipped political figures, the modern world worships political ideas. If in ancient times the radical role of the prophets was to smash the myths surrounding political figures, then modernity has added another subversive role to prophecy—to smash the myths surrounding political ideologies.

There are no perfect people, there are no perfect ideas, and there are no perfect solutions. No idea is capable of cleansing the Middle East of its violent foundations; no diplomatic initiative can extinguish hatred between peoples or religions, or impose harmony between the international community and the Jews; no political principle can redeem reality; there is no such thing as political gospel, sacred, sublime, and complete. But the concept of political humility has deep roots: it represents a fulfillment of profound and ancient Jewish prophecies.

A TRADITION OF UNDERSTANDING

One of the difficult problems of wholehearted faith in any given idea is the complete negation of all other competing ideas. Parallel to the belief that if only we implement a perfect idea, reality will be perfect runs the belief that if we implement our rivals' ideas, reality will be a catastrophe. Those who believe that their solution will bring redemption are bound to believe that their rivals' solution will bring devastation. The rhetoric of ideologies is to maintain that rival beliefs are not just wrong but dangerous. Because of this, any intellectual sphere in which perfect solutions are pitted against each other is one in which no one is listening.

As we saw at the beginning of this book, the Talmudic school of Beit Shammai refused to teach the positions of Beit Hillel. The school of Beit Hillel, however, was willing to teach the positions of Beit Shammai. Listening has a price. Whereas Beit Shammai clung stubbornly to its own positions, the scholars of Beit Hillel often backtracked in the middle of an argument, changed their minds, and ended up accepting the point of view of Beit Shammai. But ultimately, it was the rulings of Beit Hillel, not Beit Shammai, that determined the law. It was precisely those who did not insist on their own opinions, who were not dazzled by their own status, whose ideas ultimately won broad acceptance.

The tradition of the prophets urges Jews to harbor doubts about their politics, and the tradition of the Talmud urges them to harbor doubts about themselves. Jewish tradition favors not those who are always right but those who know that they are sometimes wrong. Jewish tradition is a tradition of arguing, but also one of listening—the same sort of listening that could renew and elevate Israel's culture of debate.

NOTES

Unless otherwise noted, all translations are by Eylon Levy.

INTRODUCTION

1. Babylonian Talmud, Eruvin 13b, trans. Adin Steinsaltz, in the William Davidson Talmud, Sefaria Library, Sefaria.org.
2. Ibid.
3. For further discussion, see Haim Shapira and Menachem Fish, "Polemics Between the Schools: Meta-*Halakhic* Debate Between Beit Shammai and Beit Hillel," *Tel Aviv University Law Review* 22 (1999): 461–497 [Hebrew]. This essay, which sketches the philosophical background of the debate between the two schools of thought, also touches on several cases that diverge from the norm presented above.
4. Eran Halperin, Neta Oren, and Daniel Bar-Tal, "Socio-Psychological Barriers to Resolving the Israeli-Palestinian Conflict: An Analysis of Jewish Israeli Society," in *Barriers to Peace in the Israeli-Palestinian Conflict*, ed. Yaacov Bar-Siman-Tov (Jerusalem: Jerusalem Institute for Israel Studies, 2010), 28–52.
5. For deeper analysis of the Palestinians' sense of humiliation, see Padraig O'Malley, *The Two-State Delusion: Israel and Palestine—A Tale of Two Narratives* (New York: Penguin, 2006), 22–25.
6. My presentation of the Palestinian perspective is obviously incomplete. For further reading, see Yohanan Tzoref, "Barriers to Resolution of the Conflict with Israel: The Palestinian Perspective," in *Barriers to Peace in the Israeli-Palestinian Conflict*, 58–96.

7. See the December 2013 poll conducted by the Palestinian Center for Policy and Survey Research (hereafter PCPSR), Public Opinion Poll No. 50, in which three-quarters of respondents said they would oppose a deal that included even a temporary Israeli military presence in the Jordan Valley. That said—and this point will be addressed later on—it is possible that in light of evolving regional threats, the Palestinians have an interest in an IDF presence in the Jordan Valley.

8. See the December 2014 poll conducted by the PCPSR, Joint Israeli-Palestinian Poll No. 54, according to which 53 percent of Palestinians would oppose a deal for Palestinian sovereignty in the West Bank that reserved to Israel the right to use Palestine's airspace for training exercises.

9. See Nimrod Rosler, "Fear as an Obstacle and Motive for Conflict Resolution: Theoretical Discussion and the Israeli Case," in *Barriers to Peace in the Israeli-Palestinian Conflict,* ed. Yaacov Bar-Siman-Tov (Jerusalem: Jerusalem Institute for Israel Studies, 2010), 129–157 [Hebrew]. For this essay, I used the Hebrew edition of the book, which does not precisely match the English edition. See also Daniel Bar-Tal, *Living with the Conflict: Socio-Psychological Analysis of Israeli-Jewish Society* (Jerusalem: Carmel, 2007) [Hebrew].

10. The impression among Jews that Jewish history is a never-ending tale of pogroms and persecution represents a partial reflection of historical truth. But perceptions of the past shape the present more than the past itself does. For more on the ongoing debate between historians of the Jewish people on the element of suffering in Jewish historiography, see the overview of Alon Gan, *From Victimhood to Sovereignty* (Jerusalem: Israel Democracy Institute, 2014), 171–180 [Hebrew].

11. See Tzoref, "Barriers to Resolution of the Conflict with Israel."

12. See Bernard Lewis, *What Went Wrong?* (London: Weidenfeld and Nicolson, 2002).

13. Ibid.

14. More than offense, this reality of shifting power relations has also engendered a sense of religious embarrassment. In the Islamic view, Islam's military, political, cultural, and intellectual primacy over the

West stems from God's choice of Islam as the faith that is intended to succeed the other religions and lead humanity, as well as from God's choice of the Prophet Muhammad (the "last prophet"). The transfer of this birthright to the Christian West represents not only a national but a theological challenge.

At the end of the nineteenth century, certain Muslim religious leaders—such as Jamal al-Din al-Afghani, Muhammad Abduh, and Rashid Rida—saw this situation as a divine call for Muslims to engage in comprehensive introspection, and to adopt changes and reforms in Islam. Curiously, this trend gave rise both to Islamic liberalism and to the Islamic fundamentalism that calls for a struggle against the West, from the Muslim Brotherhood through to Al Qaeda and Islamic State. For more, see Malcolm H. Kerr, *Islamic Reform: The Political and Legal Theories of Muhammad Abduh and Rashid Rida* (Berkeley: University of California Press, 1966).

15. Many factors have helped to shape the Palestinian mentality, in which Zionism is perceived as a European colonialist movement. Hillel Cohen analyzes these factors in his *Year Zero of the Arab-Israeli Conflict: 1929* (Waltham, Mass.: Brandeis University Press, 2015), presenting them clearly and methodically.

16. Akiva Yosef Schlesinger was one of the founders of Haredi Orthodoxy. Quoted in Michael Silber, "Origins of Ultra-Orthodoxy," in *Orthodox Judaism—New Perspectives,* ed. Yosef Salmon, Aviezer Ravitzky, and Adam Ferziger (Jerusalem: Magnes, 2006), 317 [Hebrew].

17. Babylonian Talmud, Berakhot 64a, trans. Adin Steinsaltz, in the William Davidson Talmud, Sefaria Library, Sefaria.org.

18. The clash of political ideologies is part of a much wider clash raging inside Israeli society, namely the rift between the religious and secular. In a later book I shall examine the intellectual roots of the debate about Israel's Jewish identity, to provide a comprehensive overview of the clash of Israeli ideas.

19. In the course of this examination, I shall use the terms *left* and *right* as generalizations. These terms will represent the traditional positions of two rival camps, while deliberately glossing over the variations within each political camp.

PART I INTRODUCTION

1. See Ehud Luz, *Parallels Meet: Religion and Nationalism in the Early Zionist Movement* (Philadelphia: Jewish Publication Society, 1988). Why did religious Jews, specifically, accept the proposal to establish a new state outside the Holy Land? There were some political and personal factors involved, such as party loyalty to the leader Theodor Herzl, but there were also religious arguments. Instead of forgetting Zion, one of the rabbis proposed a "proven remedy": to pray three times a day. See also Ehud Luz, "The Uganda Controversy," *Kivunim* 1 (1979): 59–60 [Hebrew].

2. As Eliezer Don-Yehiya has shown, Haim-Moshe Shapira led the fiercest resistance in the Israeli government against the decision to go to war. Moreover, once the messianic voices had gained traction within Religious Zionism after the conquest of Jerusalem and the territories, Shapira refrained from expressing a position on the political status of the new lands. See Eliezer Don-Yehiya, "Leadership and Policy in Religious Zionism: Chaim Moshe Shapira, the NRP and the Six-Day War," in *Religious Zionism: The Era of Change*, ed. Asher Cohen and Yisrael Harel (Jerusalem: Bialik Institute, 2004), 148–157 [Hebrew].

3. Joseph Schechtman argues that Judaism as a religion played a relatively minor part in Jabotinsky's life. Joseph Schechtman, *Rebel and Statesman: The Vladimir Jabotinsky Story* (New York: Thomas Yoseloff, 1956). This is also how Jabotinsky describes his Judaism in his autobiography; see Ze'ev Jabotinsky, "Story of My Life," in his *Collected Works,* ed. Eri Jabotinsky, 18 vols. (Jerusalem: E. Jabotinsky Ltd, 1947–1959), vol. 1: *Autobiography,* 18–19 [Hebrew]. See also Arye Naor, "'Even Heretics Have a Role at Sinai': Clarifying Jabotinsky's Relationship with Jewish Tradition," *Studies in Israeli and Modern Jewish Society* 16 (2006): 131–170 [Hebrew]; Eliezer Don-Yehiya, "Between Nationalism and Religion: The Transformation of Jabotinsky's Attitude Towards Religious Tradition," in *In the Eye of the Storm: Essays on Ze'ev Jabotinsky,* ed. Avi Bareli and Pinhas Ginossar (Sde Boker: Ben-Gurion Institute for the Study of Israel and Zionism, 2004); Michael Stanislawski, *Zionism and the Fin de Siècle: Cosmopolitanism and Nationalism from Nordau to Jabotinsky* (Berkeley: University of California Press, 2001), 116–238.

1 THE RIGHT'S IDEOLOGICAL SHIFT

1. Jabotinsky's concerns about the stability and reliability of Britain's promise were evident as early as 1918. Less than a year after the Balfour Declaration, Jabotinsky felt that the Zionist leadership headed by Chaim Weizmann was too pacifist, and that this stance was leading to the gradual erosion of Zionism's political standing. See Shmuel Katz, *Lone Wolf: A Biography of Vladimir (Ze'ev) Jabotinsky,* 2 vols. (New York: Barricade, 1996), vol. 1. See also Ze'ev Jabotinsky, "The Commandment of Pressure," *Haaretz,* 21 June 1954 [Hebrew], and "Pressure," in *The Road to Revisionist Zionism: Anthology of Essays in "Razsviet," 1923–1924,* ed. Yosef Nedava, 64–75 (Tel Aviv: Jabotinsky Institute in Israel, 1984) [Hebrew].

2. Ze'ev Jabotinsky, "Exalted Zionism—Speech at the Founding Conference of the Revisionist Zionism," Vienna, 1935, in Jabotinsky, *Collected Works,* 18 vols. ed. Eri Jabotinsky (Jerusalem: E. Jabotinsky Ltd, 1947–1959), vol. 11: *Speeches (1927–1940),* 179 [Hebrew].

    In a speech delivered in 1938, Jabotinsky spoke even more bluntly and piercingly: "I warn you without respite that the catastrophe is coming. . . . You cannot see the volcano that will soon start spewing the fire of destruction. . . . Heed my words at this midnight hour. For the love of God! May each save his own life, while time remains—and time is short! I wish to add one further word, this Ninth of Av. Those who succeed in escaping from the catastrophe will merit a moment of great Jewish joy: the rebirth and resurrection of the Jewish state. I do not know whether I shall merit this myself. Yes, my son! I believe this just as surely as I believe that tomorrow morning the sun will rise again. I believe this with total faith"; Ze'ev Jabotinsky, "In the Spirit of the Ninth of Av," in Jabotinsky, *Guiding Principles for the Problems of the Day,* ed. Yosef Nedava (Tel Aviv: Jabotinsky Institute in Israel, 1981), 160 [Hebrew]. In a speech given the following year, Jabotinsky tried to frighten the crowd, warning, "Destruction. Destruction. Repeat this word out loud, and I hope that *I* shall be wrong"; Jabotinsky, "The End of Hollow Condemnations," ibid., 164 [Hebrew].

3. One note of reservation: there is disagreement among experts about

whether Jabotinsky in fact envisioned the systematic extermination
of European Jewry as wrought by Nazi Germany or whether he
meant to warn of a more general danger—the political downfall and
social collapse of European Jewry, which would necessarily lead to
assimilation.

For scholars who view Jabotinsky as a man who foresaw the
true nature of the coming calamity, see Katz, *Lone Wolf*, vol. 2; Yosef
Nedava, "Foreseeing Events and a Feeling for the Holocaust," *In the
Dispersion of Exile* 19, nos. 83–84 (1978): 100–107 [Hebrew]; Benzion
Netanyahu, *The Founding Fathers of Zionism* (New York: Gefen, 2012).

For the more moderate and skeptical interpretation, see Yaakov
Shavit and Liat Shteir-Livni, "Who Cried Wolf? How Did Ze'ev Jabotinsky Understand the Nature and Intentions of Nazi Germany?" in *In
the Eye of the Storm: Essays on Ze'ev Jabotinsky*, ed. Avi Bareli and Pinhas
Ginossar (Sde Boker: Ben-Gurion Institute for the Study of Israel
and Zionism, 2004); Yaacov Shavit, *The Mythologies of the Zionist Right
Wing* (Tzofit: Beit-Berl and the Moshe Sharett Institute, 1986), 63–84
[Hebrew]; Dan Michman, "Ze'ev Jabotinsky: The Evocation Plan and
the Problem of Foreseeing the Holocaust," *Kivunim* 7 (May 1980):
119–127 [Hebrew]. See also the discussion of Jabotinsky and comprehensive summary in Amir Goldstein, ed., *Zionism and Anti-Semitism
in the Thought and Action of Ze'ev Jabotinsky* (Sde Boker: Ben-Gurion
University Press and Jabotinsky Institute in Israel, 2015), 424–440
[Hebrew].

4. See for example Jabotinsky, speech at the Zionist General Council,
"The Security of the Yishuv—the Foundational Question of Zionism,"
in Jabotinsky, *Collected Works*, vol. 10: *Speeches (1905–1926)*, 189–207
[Hebrew]. Jabotinsky compares the Arab riots to the pogroms in
Europe. He considers them both expressions of anti-Semitism, be-
lieving there is no reason to attempt persuasion or dialogue; ibid., 97
[Hebrew].

5. Such was the position of Theodor Herzl, illustrated most clearly in
his utopian novel *Altneuland* (Old New Land). For a more thorough
analysis of Herzl's position, see Derek Penslar, "Herzl and the Palestinian Arabs: Myths and Counter-Myths," *Journal of Israeli History* 24,

no. 1 (2005): 65–77. For more on the positions of Herzl, Jabotinsky, and other Zionist thinkers on the question of their relationship with the Arabs, see Yosef Gorni, *Zionism and the Arabs, 1882–1948: A Study of Ideology* (Oxford: Clarendon, 1987).

6. Jabotinsky, "On the Iron Wall" (1923), an essay that was originally published in Russian; my translation is based on the Hebrew version available at the Jabotinsky Institute website. Jabotinsky's warnings were implicitly directed at the official Zionist leaders, particularly Chaim Weizmann and Nahum Sokolow, who believed that it was possible to reach an agreement and a compromise with the Arab leaders. See Joseph Heller, "The Positions of Ben-Gurion, Weizmann, and Jabotinsky on the Arab Question: Comparative Study," in *The Zionist Age*, ed. Anita Shapira, Jehuda Reinharz, and Jacob Harris (Jerusalem: Zalman Shazar Centre, 2000), 233–234 [Hebrew]; Arye Naor, "'From the Wealth of Our Land There Shall Prosper': On Ze'ev Jabotinsky's Relationship to the Arabs of the Land of Israel," in *Nationalism and Morality: Zionist Discourse and the Arab Question*, ed. Ephraim Lavie (Jerusalem: Carmel, 2014), 123–142 [Hebrew].

7. Jabotinsky even argued that the Arabs themselves saw him as the only Zionist who truly understood them: "Some of the Arabs addressed me, and they did so in a curious manner. They wrote in a letter, 'You are the only Zionist who does not want to deceive us, and who understands that the Arab is a patriot and not a whore.'" Ze'ev Jabotinsky, "After Establishing the Border Corps" (1926), in Jabotinsky, *Collected Works*, 10:303 [Hebrew].

8. "The tragedy is such," Jabotinsky continued in "After Establishing the Border Corps," "that there lies herein a collision between two truths . . . and this tragedy cannot bequeath us a possibility for peace. There is no room for peace"; ibid.

9. Ze'ev Jabotinsky, "*Homo Homini Lupus*" (1910), in Jabotinsky, *Collected Works*, vol. 2: *Nation and Society*, 256 [Hebrew].

10. Ibid.

11. See Ze'ev Jabotinsky, "I Do Not Believe" (1910) and "Rights and Violence" (1911), in Jabotinsky, *Collected Works*, vol. 15: *Feuilletons*, 81–105 [Hebrew].

12. For Jabotinsky's militaristic worldview, see in particular "On Militarism" (1933) and "On the Brother" (1933) in Jabotinsky, *Collected Works*, vol. 4: *On the Road to Statehood*, 39–58, 85–95 [Hebrew].

13. Raphaella Bilski Ben-Hur has conducted extensive research on this matter. See Raphaella Bilski Ben-Hur, *Every Individual, a King: The Social and Political Thought of Ze'ev Vladimir Jabotinsky* (Washington, D.C.: Bnai Brith Books, 1993). See also *Ze'ev Jabotinsky, To the Essence of Democracy: The Liberal and Democratic Philosophy of Ze'ev Jabotinsky* (Tel Aviv: Jabotinsky Medal, 2001) [Hebrew].

14. Jabotinsky, "Story of My Life," in Jabotinsky, *Collected Works*, vol. 1: *Autobiography*, 38 [Hebrew].

15. I must include one reservation to this identification: Jabotinsky's liberal statements are certainly decisive—but he also made other, more illiberal remarks. Jabotinsky espoused an organic theory of nationalism: the nation is a living being, with a discernible nature and distinct character. If the nation is an organic entity, then each of the nation's individuals is an organ in a larger body. This theory, of course, is deeply illiberal. Organic nationalist philosophy tends not to go together with liberal political philosophy. But for Jabotinsky, the two went hand-in-hand. Despite his organic nationalism, in which individuals were identified as belonging to the collective (the nation), Jabotinsky's ideal *state* was a liberal one, in which the individual did not belong to the state, and each and every person was a king, pursuing individual self-actualization.

Jabotinsky's philosophy of the *nation*, that is, did not shape his philosophy of the *state*. Both these elements found expression in his theory of Zionism, in which the State of Israel would be the place in which the Jewish national corpus could flourish. But that same state would be liberal, nurturing the individualism of every citizen. In modern-day Israel, too, Jabotinsky's theory of nationalism does not need to shape an individual's political philosophy. As a state, Israel can nurture the special character of the Jewish people while remaining obligated equally to all its citizens, including its Arab citizens.

This contradiction in Jabotinsky's thought preoccupies historians and researchers of Jabotinsky, who disagree about what he propounded. Scholars such as Shlomo Avineri, Gideon Shimoni, and Shalom Ratzabi have emphasized Jabotinsky's militarism, discipline, monism, and ethno-nationalism in order to demonstrate the way his outlook was influenced by the integral nationalism that flourished at the time in Europe. In contrast, researchers such as Raphaella Bilski Ben-Hur and Arye Naor stress the liberal and democratic aspects of Jabotinsky's thought, his profound belief in individualism and basic equality, while depicting the other elements as marginal, momentary digressions, or not necessarily in opposition to his fundamentally liberal credo.

See Shlomo Avineri, *The Making of Modern Zionism: The Intellectual Origins of the Jewish State* (New York: Basic, 1981); Gideon Shimoni, *The Zionist Ideology* (Hanover, N.H.: University Press of New England, 1995); Shalom Ratzabi, "Race, Nation and Judaism in M. M. Buber's and Z. Jabotinsky's Thought," in *In the Eye of the Storm*, 121–158; Bilski Ben-Hur, *Every Individual, a King*; Arye Naor, "In the Beginning, God Created: Individual and Society in Jabotinsky's Thought," in Ze'ev Jabotinsky, *Ideological Writings*, vol. 1: *Liberal Nationalism*, ed. Arye Naor (Tel Aviv: Jabotinsky Institute in Israel, 2012), 11–56 [Hebrew]; Shavit, *Mythologies of the Zionist Right Wing*, 208–209 [Hebrew]; Zeev Tzahor, "Jabotinsky and Jabotinskyism," in *In the Eye of the Storm*, 39–50.

I am grateful to Eliran Zered for introducing me to this fascinating controversy.

16. Jabotinsky, "Story of My Life," 38 [Hebrew]. Jabotinsky described a kind of utopian society in one of his stories, "The Truth About the Island of Tristan da Runha," in Jabotinsky, *Collected Works*, 2:367–392 [Hebrew]. For an analysis of this story, see Svetlana Natkovich, *Among Radiant Clouds* (Jerusalem: Magnes, 2015), 174–178 [Hebrew]; Svetlana Natkovich, "A Land of Harsh Ways: 'Tristan da Runha' as Jabotinsky's Social Fantasy," *Jewish Social Studies* 19, no. 2 (2012): 24–49.

17. Jabotinsky the liberal understood that democracy embraces not merely majority rule; it primarily demands the defense of minorities against the tyranny of the majority: "Nevertheless, the blind iden-

tification of democracy with majority rule is in fact incorrect. The value of democracy does not hinge on the feeling of subjugation of forty-nine equal kings to one hundred, nor even to ten, nor even one to a hundred." Jabotinsky, "Introduction to Economic Theory (B)," in Jabotinsky, *Collected Works,* 2:219 [Hebrew].

In a different article, Jabotinsky posits two tests for a genuine democracy: "First, in any given country, is the individual considered the sovereign, and his freedom the height of legislation, and is the state's authority to limit his freedom permitted only in cases of strict necessity—or, conversely, is this a state in which the citizen is foremost a subject, and does the state demand for itself the right to direct every aspect of its citizens' lives and activities? And second, does this state protect the freedom of everyone who publicly criticizes the government of the day, or is this right denied? These two criteria are sufficient to distinguish between democracy and its opposite, whatever might be written in the constitution." Jabotinsky, "Perspectives on Problems in State and Society" (1940), in Jabotinsky, *Guiding Principles for the Problems of the Day,* 22 [Hebrew]. See a rehearsal of this idea in Jabotinsky, "Sons of Kings," *HaMashkif,* 25 April 1941, and "The Social Question," *HaYarden,* 21 October 1938.

18. Ze'ev Jabotinsky, "Israel's Land" (1929), in Jabotinsky, *Guiding Principles for the Problems of the Day,* 75 [Hebrew]. Later, Jabotinsky even interprets the lyrics of his famous "Shir Betar" [The Betar Song]: "Even in poverty a Jew is a prince / Whether slave or tramp / You have been created the son of kings / Crowned with the diadem of David / Whether in light or in darkness / Always remember the crown / The crown of pride and Tagar": "I, who wrote these words, intended to apply them to every single person, Greek or Bantu, northern or Eskimo. All were created in the image of God." Ze'ev Jabotinsky, "Perspectives on Problems in State and Society" (1940), ibid., 20 [Hebrew]. The translation of "Shir Betar" is from "The Betar Song," at hebrewsongs.com (http://hebrewsongs.com/?song=shirbetar).

19. Ze'ev Jabotinsky, "The Arab Problem—Without Dramatics" (1940), in Jabotinsky, *Guiding Principles for the Problems of the Day,* 105 [Hebrew].

See also Arye Naor, "Jabotinsky's Constitutional Guidelines for Israel," in *In the Eye of the Storm,* 51–92.

20. One can certainly disagree with this blunt conclusion and aver that while Jabotinsky's political Zionism is based on *his* understanding of the international community's promise, that understanding was only one possible, rather than a necessary, reading of that commitment. The Balfour Declaration did not say that Palestine would *be* the national home of the Jewish people but rather that the national home of the Jewish people would be established *in* Palestine. This phrasing left room for the creation of additional polities on the soil of Palestine. See Uri Naaman and David Arbel, *Borderline Choices* (Tel Aviv: Yediot Books, 2011), 16–17 [Hebrew].

Arye Naor emphasizes the legalistic and symbolic relationship of Jabotinsky's Revisionist movement with the Land of Israel, differing from that of the Labor Zionist movement. He distinguishes between the two aspects of Jabotinsky's approach to the Land of Israel—one instrumental and legalistic, the other expressive and symbolic. In the first sense, which Naor assesses as the more dominant, the Land of Israel serves as the appropriate vessel for the Zionist goal of absorbing masses of Jews from the Diaspora and providing them with a safe haven, as Theodor Herzl understood it. Here we see the mathematical-demographic aspect of Jabotinsky's thought, in which Jabotinsky calculates population figures and territory with an eye on economic viability. See for example his essays "On the Iron Wall" and "The Arab Problem—Without Dramatics," as well as his "Fulfill Your Promise; or, Get Out of the Mandate! Testimony at the Royal Commission" (1937), in Jabotinsky, *Collected Works,* vol. 5: *In Times of Wrath,* 221–271 [Hebrew].

In the second aspect of Jabotinsky's approach, he ascribes to the land a certain holiness as an intrinsic value but not in the religious sense of a divine promise. Instead, the sense is mythical and historical, inasmuch as the Jewish people were native and indigenous to the land, had lived there, had fought for it, and had yearned for it for thousands of years. See among other writings Ze'ev Jabotinsky, "Zionism and the Land of Israel," in Jabotinsky, *Collected Works,* vol.

8: *First Zionist Writings,* 107–129 [Hebrew], and his poem "The East Bank of the Jordan," in *Collected Works,* 2:21–22 [Hebrew]. See also Arye Naor, "On the Matter of the Land of Israel in Revisionist Zionist Thought: Political Theology and Instrumental Considerations," in *The Land of Israel in Modern Jewish Thought,* ed. Aviezer Ravitzky (Jerusalem: Yad Yitzhak Ben-Zvi, 1998), 422–495 [Hebrew]; Naor, "It's All Mine! The Land of Israel in Jabotinsky's Thought," in Jabotinsky, *Ideological Writings,* 1:9–35 [Hebrew]; Jabotinsky, *The Land of Israel A* (Jerusalem: Jabotinsky Institute in Israel, 2015), 9–35 [Hebrew]; Naor, "Greater Israel Ideology and Politics in the Revisionist Movement, 1925–1948," *Contemporary Jewry* 14 (2000): 9–41 [Hebrew].

Yaacov Shavit advances an even more extreme position than Naor, arguing that Jabotinsky's worldview was entirely pragmatic, without a shred of romanticism; Shavit, *Mythologies of the Zionist Right Wing,* 216 [Hebrew]; see also Shavit, "Ze'ev Jabotinsky: Between Liberal Nationalism and Romantic Nationalism," *Gesher* 144 (2001): 27–36 [Hebrew]. This impression is strengthened by Jabotinsky's own remarks in his "Story of My Life": "I had no romantic love for the Land of Israel then, and I am not sure whether that will change now" (49) [Hebrew].

21. Jabotinsky's Zionism was a brand of political Zionism. He saw Theodor Herzl as his spiritual father and the source of the inspiration for his ideas. According to Herzl, the Jewish state would be founded neither through the settlement of the land nor through military force: the state of the Jews would be established through international agreement. At the First Zionist Congress, held in Basel, Switzerland, in 1897, Herzl declared that the goal of Zionism was "a publicly recognised and legally secured home in Palestine for the Jewish people"; *The Congress Addresses of Theodor Herzl,* trans. Nellie Straus (New York: Federation of American Zionists, 1917). The State of Israel was meant to be the achievement neither of settlement nor of military strength.

Regarding the purpose of militarism, Jabotinsky was in disagreement with his own disciples. Jabotinsky favored a powerful Jewish military force, capable of self-defense. He also believed that militarism would rehabilitate the diasporic character of the Jews. But militarism was never intended as a substitute for diplomacy—only as a precondition for it. The Hebrew battalions in World War I, for example, were formed in order to urge the British to grant the Jews a state. The cultivation of a strong military force, Jabotinsky believed, would enhance the political will of the British to fulfill the Balfour Declaration.

But those of Jabotinsky's followers who founded the Lehi (Stern Gang), for example—a paramilitary group that operated between 1940 and 1948—believed that the State of Israel could arise through military force alone. Similarly, Jabotinsky's heir and successor, Menachem Begin, believed that the State of Israel could be established only by means of a military revolt, not political agreement. In 1938, at the Third World Congress of the Betar Movement, the Revisionist Zionist youth movement, Begin challenged Jabotinsky's leadership, demanding that the group move away from a diplomatic Zionism that retained faith in the conscience of the international community and toward a militarist Zionism. Jabotinsky delivered a searing rebuttal. He blasted Begin's speech. See Daniel Gordis, *Menachem Begin: The Battle for Israel's Soul* (New York: Schocken, 2014), 24.

But in accordance with this new worldview, Begin proposed amending the wording of the Betar oath. Jabotinsky's formula read, "Only in defense will I raise my hand." Begin's proposed amendment read, "I will prepare my hand for the defense of my people and the conquest of my homeland." In the end, not only was the formula amended as Begin demanded, but the Irgun (also known as the Etzel, a paramilitary group later absorbed into the IDF) followed Begin's command too. When he became commander of the Irgun, Begin declared a revolt against the British. This military force ultimately subsumed the diplomatic effort it was originally intended to serve; ibid., 24 (quotations); Ofer Grosbard, *Menachem Begin—The Absent Leader* (Haifa: IDF National Defense College, 2007).

22. This belief in the power of the international community was the basis for Jabotinsky's political doctrine of pressure. He was a fervent believer in diplomacy, in a form that would rely not only on political and economic leverage but on trust in the conscience of the world community as well. This stands in stark contradiction to his suspicious

and violent understanding of human nature and society. Shlomo Avineri emphasizes this difficult paradox between Jabotinsky's demands of moral action in his diplomatic meetings and his realist conception of politics as based on force in *The Making of Modern Zionism.*

23. Menachem Begin led a withdrawal from the Sinai Peninsula, but he did not view it as a step back from Jabotinsky's philosophy. The Sinai had never been included in the borders of the British Mandate—and in Jabotinsky's mind, the borders of the Promised Land were the borders of the British Mandate. See Aryeh Eldad, *Things You See from Here* (Or Yehuda: Kinneret, 2016), 38–39, 97–134 [Hebrew].

24. One of the key differences between Begin and Jabotinsky was that Begin turned the divine promise into one of the right wing's core justifications for Greater Israel. The day after the U.N. vote on partition, Begin said over the radio: "On behalf of the divine promise made to the father of our nation . . . the partition of our homeland is illegal. It shall never be recognized. . . . The Land of Israel shall be restored to the Jewish people. All of it. Forever." Menachem Begin, "The Day After the U.N. Resolution: The Sanctity of the Wholeness of the Homeland," in Begin, *In the Underground: Writings, Volume D* (Tel Aviv: Hadar, 1977), 80 [Hebrew].

    For an elaboration of these differences, see Arye Naor, "Greater Israel Ideology and Politics in the Revisionist Movement" [Hebrew]; Naor, "Religion and Nation in the Worldview of the Zionist Right: From Jabotinsky to Begin," in *Jewish Identity,* ed. Asher Maoz and Aviad Hacohen (Tel Aviv: Tel Aviv University Buchmann Faculty of Law, 2013), 251–290 [Hebrew].

25. See Gordis, *Menachem Begin;* Mordechai Kremnitzer and Amir Fuchs, *Menachem Begin on Democracy and Constitutional Values* (Jerusalem: Israel Democracy Institute, 2012).

26. In 1978, Menachem Begin was adamant during the negotiations with Anwar El Sadat that led to the Camp David Accords that he would not relinquish Judea and Samaria. During his time in office, the settlement enterprise gained powerful and impressive momentum—and all the while Begin continued to fortify the rule of law, gave respectful deference to the High Court, and safeguarded human rights.

27. This phenomenon is investigated in depth in Gil Samsonov, *The Princes* (Or Yehuda: Dvir, 2015) [Hebrew]. See also Yechiam Weitz, "Princes of Hadar," in his *Between Ze'ev Jabotinsky and Menachem Begin: Essays on the Revisionist Movement* (Jerusalem: Magnes, 2012), 236–246 [Hebrew].

28. Samsonov, *The Princes,* 14–16 [Hebrew]. Samsonov explains that while familial dynasties exist all around the world, there is no precedent for intergenerational political dynasties of this form.

29. For the political dispute among the princes and their ultimate fragmentation, see Samsonov, *The Princes,* 268ff.

30. As soon as the Six-Day War ended, some Israelis—such as Finance Minister Pinchas Sapir and the public intellectual Yeshayahu Leibowitz—began warning about the demographic problem, but they represented a minority on the margins of public debate. Public awareness of the demographic problem became widespread only in the 1980s, when it first entered the consciousness of many Israelis. See Uriel Abulof, *Living on the Edge: The Existential Uncertainty of Zionism* (Haifa: Yediot Books and Haifa University Press, 2015), 81–82 [Hebrew].

31. Some demographers dispute these calculations, and I shall discuss the debate between the demographers in Part II, in the chapter "No Demographic Problem?"

32. See "Prime Minister Ariel Sharon's Address to the Knesset Prior to the Vote on the Disengagement Plan (October 25, 2004)," at www .knesset.gov.il/docs/eng/sharonspeech04.htm.

33. See, for example, Ehud Olmert's speech at the Herzliya Conference, January 2006 (the full speech appears at the conference website: www.herzliyaconference.org); Tzipi Livni's remarks at the Israeli Presidential Conference in Jerusalem, October 2009, in Pinhas Wolf, "Livni: In 2020, Israel Is Set to Lose Its Demographic Majority," Walla News (22 October 2009), available at News.walla.co.il/item/1594439 (accessed on 26 October 2016) [Hebrew].

34. In the speech Netanyahu announced: "But, friends, we must state the whole truth here. The truth is that in the area of our homeland, in the heart of our Jewish Homeland, now lives a large population of Palestinians. We do not want to rule over them. We do not want to

run their lives. We do not want to force our flag and our culture on them. In my vision of peace, there are two free peoples living side by side in this small land, with good neighbourly relations and mutual respect." "Full Text of Netanyahu's Foreign Policy Speech at Bar Ilan University," *Haaretz,* 14 June 2009.

35. For an elaboration on the complicated relationship between Jabotinsky and the maximalist wing of the Revisionist movement, see Eran Kaplan, *The Jewish Radical Right: Revisionist Zionism and Its Ideological Legacy* (Madison: University of Wisconsin Press, 2005), 3–30; Yaacov Shavit, *Jabotinsky and the Revisionist Movement* (London: Cass, 1988), 107–161.

36. In his speech at the Herzliya Conference, Olmert even quoted Jabotinsky concerning the centrality of the majority principle in his philosophy of liberalism and maximalism.

37. Ze'ev Jabotinsky, letter to the editor of the *Jewish Chronicle,* a Jewish newspaper published in Britain, 12 June 1925. Jabotinsky included other illuminating insights in his essay "Majority" (1923), in his *Collected Works,* 4:195–203 [Hebrew]. In this essay, Jabotinsky calls for a "return to basics . . . first and foremost: the creation of a Jewish majority is, has always been, and will remain the foundational purpose of Zionism" (197). The majority principle was a dominant component of all Jabotinsky's public statements on the goals of Zionism, synonymous for him with "the state of the Jews." "What is the practical meaning of 'Jewish state'?" he wrote in Betar's document of principles in 1934. "The first condition for a nation state is a national majority." Jabotinsky, "The Idea of Betar," ibid., 4:310 [Hebrew].

38. *Jabotinsky's World—Anthology of Statements and Theoretical Principles,* ed. Moshe Bila (Dfusim: Tel Aviv, 1972) [Hebrew].

39. This is why Jabotinsky opposed the establishment of a democratic parliament for the residents of the Land of Israel during the British Mandate period. He believed that the civilian population such a parliament should represent included the Jews who would immigrate in future, in line with the purpose of the Mandate. Ze'ev Jabotinsky, "In the Land of Israel Congress" (1919), in Jabotinsky, *Collected Works,* 10:97 [Hebrew].

40. Jabotinsky, "Israel's Land," 75 [Hebrew].

41. To be precise, the reliance on a promise by God rather than the international community already existed in the thinking of the Lehi, as was also evident in Menachem Begin's speeches. See Naor, "Greater Israel Ideology and Politics in the Revisionist Movement," 9–41 [Hebrew].

42. One clarification needs to be made: one foundational pillar of the Israeli right has remained intact—its suspicious political outlook, along with an understanding that nothing can be relied upon but independent military strength. This conservative security axiom was present in Jabotinsky's philosophy, as we have seen, and it continues to characterize the political thought of the religious right. In the course of the book, we shall see that since the disengagement from Gaza in 2005, this principle has gained strength at the expense of the messianic principle.

2 THE LEFT'S IDEOLOGICAL SHIFT

1. A clarification needs to be made: the lack of faith in the possibility of reaching a political resolution to Israel's relationship with the Arab world was a dominant theme in the labor movement, but it was by no means the only theme. The Labor politician Yigal Allon, for example, presented an alternative vision, in which Israel should aspire to transform its political standing, to liberate itself from the status quo, and to strive for a peace agreement with the Arabs. For the differences between the two left-wing schools, see Udi Manor, *Yigal Allon: Political Biography, 1949–1980* (Or Yehuda: Dvir, 2016), 25–29 [Hebrew].

2. Moshe Dayan, "Not from the Arabs but Ourselves We Seek Roy's Blood," *Davar,* 2 May 1956 [Hebrew]; Dayan, *A New Map, New Relationships* (Tel Aviv: Maariv Press, 1969) [Hebrew].

3. Shimon Peres, *David's Sling* (New York: Random House, 1970), 9–10.

4. Conversely, some scholars argue that Egypt was not ready to reach an agreement and deliberately made offers that Israel could not accept. For elaboration, see Boaz Vanetik and Zaki Shalom, "The White House Middle East Policy in 1973 as a Catalyst for the Outbreak of

the Yom Kippur War," *Israel Studies* 16, no. 1 (Spring 2011): 53–78. See also Yigal Kipnis, *1973: The Road to War* (Charlottesville, Va.: Just World Books, 2013), especially the introductory chapter.

5. Karl Marx and Friedrich Engels, *The Communist Manifesto* (Auckland, N.Z.: Floating Press, 2008), 6.

6. For strong evidence of this shift, consider the emergence of the Meretz Party. Meretz was established as a merger between various factions that clashed on socioeconomic issues but shared a common view on diplomatic policy. On the one hand was the Mapam, the kibbutz-led United Workers Party; on another was Ratz, the Movement for Civil Rights and Peace, founded by members of the Tel Aviv bourgeoisie; and on yet another was a section of Shinui (Change; a centrist secular party), which advocated for free-market liberalization. A political party based on an alliance between socialism and capitalism would have been unthinkable in the first few decades of Israel's existence, but by the early 1990s this alliance had come to seem almost natural. The political merger that formed Meretz illustrates that for the modern left, the political-diplomatic question takes precedence over every other consideration.

7. The U.S.-Israel relationship experienced ups and downs in its early years, but the special relationship between the two countries stabilized after 1967, and especially after 1973. See Avraham Ben-Zvi, *From Truman to Obama* (Tel Aviv: Yediot Books, 2011) [Hebrew].

8. The government unanimously approved the following resolution: "Israel is offering to forge peace with Egypt [and Syria] based on the international border and Israel's security requirements." See the Israeli government meeting protocols, 19 June 1967, at the Israel State Archives, the Six-Day War files, available at http://www.archives.gov .il/archives/#/Archive/0b0717068031be30/File/0b0717068212c55b/ Item/0907170682de093d.

9. One reservation needs to be noted: the peace movement that arose at the end of the 1980s was not unprecedented. Yaakov Hazan, one of the leaders of the Hashomer Hatzair youth movement, had declared peace to be one of the goals of Zionism: "Peace with the Arabs is the guarantee of our existence in the Land of Israel. For us, this is a func-

tion of socialism and an imperative of Zionism."; see Shmuel Dota, *The Debate over Partition During the Mandate Era* (Jerusalem: Ben-Zvi Institute, 1979), 142 [Hebrew]. In the 1920s and 1930s, the Yishuv saw the emergence of several movements and organizations—the most prominent was Brit Shalom—whose members saw peace with the inhabitants of the land as a goal of the movement whose purpose was to settle the land.

But these voices represented a minority opinion, on the margins of the Zionist movement. Peace began to take its first steps from the political periphery toward the center in the years between the Six-Day War and the Yom Kippur War. This was when Yaakov Rotblit wrote his "Shir LaShalom" (Song for Peace), whose lyrics included this plea: "Bring about the day!" Intellectuals such as Amos Oz and Yeshayahu Leibowitz called for an end to the occupation of the territories. But their voices remained at the edge of public discourse in these interwar years.

Moshe Dayan's exhortation that "we have returned to the holiest of our holy places, never to part from it again" was a more accurate representation of the mood of the day. The change in direction took place only after the Yom Kippur War, and mostly came about after the peace process with Egypt began. (For Dayan, see "40th Anniversary of the Reunification of Jerusalem," Israel Ministry of Foreign Affairs website, at http://www.mfa.gov.il/mfa/aboutisrael/state/jerusalem/pages/40th%20anniversary%20of%20the%20reunification%20of%20jerusalem.aspx.)

10. For more on the difficulties in negotiations see Daniel Gordis, *Menachem Begin: The Battle for Israel's Soul* (New York: Schocken, 2014).

11. At the outset of the 1980s, a war erupted that would ignite the optimistic fervor of the Israeli peace camp: the Lebanon War. It began as a limited campaign to push terrorists away from Israel's northern border, and it initially received widespread public support. But as time went on, the war continued to expand. As it became more protracted, the national consensus in Israel shrank and dwindled away. The more the IDF became bogged down in the "mud of Lebanon," the louder the protest against the war grew. Thus, the peace move-

ment that emerged out of hope for a continued peace evolved into a protest movement against an ongoing war.

12. Shimon Peres, *The New Middle East* (New York: Henry Holt, 1993).

13. I must include this reservation to my claim of a shift: the ideas of socialism and peace were connected in the early days of Zionism, when people sporadically believed that solidarity among Hebrew workers would spread into solidarity among all workers, including Arabs. The fulfillment of the socialist vision would thus also mean the realization of the dream of peace. See Anita Shapira, *Berl: The Biography of a Socialist Zionist, Berl Katznelson* (New York: Cambridge University Press, 1984).

   That said, we would be hard-pressed to say that this idea was central to left-wing ideology at the time. Over the years, the causes of socialism and peace did not become intertwined. Ultimately, socialism failed to produce peace and was itself replaced by the ideology of peace. For an honest discussion of this ideological shift with two of the founders of the modern left, Yossi Sarid and Yossi Beilin, see Ari Shavit, *My Promised Land: The Triumph and Tragedy of Israel* (New York: Spiegel and Grau, 2015), 239–270.

14. See Asher Arian, "A Further Turn to the Right: Israeli Public Opinion on National Security," *INSS Strategic Assessment* 5, no. 1 (June 2002): 19–24.

15. Ibid.

16. To clarify, this description is a conventional account of the failure of the Camp David summit. The accepted narrative is that the summit collapsed because of Palestinian rejectionism. While I personally find this version of events compelling, alternative accounts apportion the blame among all sides at the talks, while other competing narratives pin all the blame on Israel. For a summary of the different accounts, see Itamar Rabinovich, *The Lingering Conflict: Israel, the Arabs, and the Middle East, 1948–2012* (Washington, D.C.: Brookings Institution Press, 2012); see also Padraig O'Malley, *The Two-State Delusion: Israel and Palestine—A Tale of Two Narratives* (New York: Penguin, 2006), 90–96.

17. There is disagreement within the Israeli intelligence community as to whether Arafat deliberately initiated the Second Intifada (as the Military

Intelligence Directorate's Research Department maintains) or whether he joined in the larger Arab uprising later (as argued by sections of the Military Intelligence Directorate and the Israel Security Agency).

18. In the narrative widespread among Palestinians and cadres of the Israeli and European left, the opposite is true. In this narrative, the bulk of the blame for the outbreak of the Second Intifada falls on the Israelis. How so? The Oslo Accords raised expectations among the Palestinian public even as in parallel to this political process settlement activity soared, the settler population rose, new roads were paved across the territories, and Israel signaled through its deeds that the country was not interested in ending the occupation but rather sought to expand it. The gulf between expectations and reality resulted in a major grievance that erupted in the form of the Second Intifada.

   The great majority of Israelis blame the Palestinians for the violence of the Second Intifada, in contrast to how they view the First Intifada. See Eran Halperin, Neta Oren, and Daniel Bar-Tal, "Socio-Psychological Barriers to Resolving the Israeli-Palestinian Conflict: An Analysis of Jewish Israeli Society," in *Barriers to Peace in the Israeli-Palestinian Conflict,* ed. Yaacov Bar-Siman-Tov (Jerusalem: Jerusalem Institute for Israel Studies, 2010).

   It is worth adding that whereas for Israelis the word *occupation* generally refers to the military rule over noncitizen Palestinians that began in 1967, the Palestinians use the term to refer to the establishment of the State of Israel itself and to Israeli sovereignty from 1948 on. As such, "ending the occupation" means something very different for Israelis to what it means for Palestinians.

19. Ari Shavit, "Israeli-Palestinian Peace Is Dead, Long Live Peace," *Haaretz,* 22 September 2014.

20. I am grateful to my friend Yossi Klein Halevi for this illuminating distinction.

21. This poll is taken from Uriel Abulof, *Living on the Edge: The Existential Uncertainty of Zionism* (Haifa: Yediot Books and Haifa University Press, 2015), 85, 118 [Hebrew]. See also the in-depth polls described ibid., 259.

3 RELIGIOUS ZIONISM AND THE MESSIANIC SHIFT

1. Eliezer Don-Yehiya demonstrates that there were indications as early as the 1950s of the new spirit of Religious Zionism, but it did not find political expression in the policy of the Mizrahi Party. See Eliezer Don-Yehiya, "Leadership and Policy in Religious Zionism: Chaim Moshe Shapira, the NRP and the Six-Day War," in *Religious Zionism: The Era of Change,* ed. Asher Cohen and Yisrael Harel (Jerusalem: Bialik Institute, 2004), 135–170 [Hebrew].

2. See Aviezer Ravitzky, *Messianism, Zionism, and Jewish Religious Radicalism* (Tel Aviv: Am Oved, 1993), 170–172 [Hebrew].

3. To what extent was Rabbi Zvi Yehuda the true successor of his father, Rabbi Kook? His disciples considered him the most authoritative commentator on his father's writings, but the academic community is more skeptical. Professor Benjamin Ish-Shalom, for example, focuses his research on Rabbi Kook the elder rather than on his son and other disciples using the argument that "we know that on questions of principle, they diverged from his path." Benjamin Ish-Shalom, "Religious Zionism—Between Apologia and Coping," *Cathedra* 90 (December 1988): 148 [Hebrew].

    Aviezer Ravitzky has also pointed out substantive differences between the two men: "Rabbi Kook's messianic faith and optimistic expectations of the future assumed, among his disciples, a solid veneer of messianic certainty and foreknowledge of the future." Ravitzky, *Messianism, Zionism, and Jewish Religious Radicalism,* 172 [Hebrew].

    On the other hand, some academics have argued that Rabbi Kook and his disciples (Rabbi Zvi Yehuda, the "Nazirite" Rabbi David Cohen, and Rabbi Yaakov Moshe Charlap) should be considered as constituting a single school of thought that contains differences but is best studied as a whole, in light of the continuity between Rabbi Kook and the disciples, and their dependence on him. This argument was first made by Dov Schwartz in "Paths in the Study of Religious Zionist Thought," in *Ayin Tova—Dialogue and Polemic in Jewish Culture: Jubilee Book in Honor of Tova Ilan,* ed. Yosef Ahituv et al. (Tel Aviv: Hakibbutz Hameuchad, 1999), 564–581 [Hebrew], and elsewhere, and later by Jonathan Garb, Uriel Barak, and others.

The revolutionary shift that changed the face of Religious Zionism in the 1970s was pioneered by the spiritual leadership of the Merkaz HaRav Yeshiva and its graduates. Gideon Aran has shown that the seeds of this major shift were planted as early as the 1950s, when Religious Zionists began to discover the Merkaz HaRav Yeshiva when they were members of the Pioneering Torah Scholar Group, also known as *Gahlat.* See Gideon Aran, *Kookism* (Jerusalem: Carmel, 2013), 30–109 [Hebrew].

4. The statement first appeared in an article in the newspaper *HaTzofe* (The Observer), 26 January 1975, and is quoted in Ravitzky, *Messianism, Zionism, and Jewish Religious Radicalism,* 113 [Hebrew].

5. See Dov Schwartz, *Challenge and Crisis in Rabbi Kook's Circle* (Tel Aviv: Am Oved, 2002), 56–86 [Hebrew].

6. Rabbi Zvi Yehuda Kook, *On the Ways of Israel* (*Lintivot Yisrael*), Section A, pp. 193–194 [Hebrew], quoted in Ravitzky, *Messianism, Zionism, and Jewish Religious Radicalism,* 113 [Hebrew]. Rabbi Zvi Yehuda's seminal essay, "The State as the Fulfillment of the Redemptive Vision," in his *On the Ways of Israel* [Hebrew], interprets the events surrounding Israel's establishment in the context of the broader historical drama of redemption.

7. Asked whether he and his students were transgressing the Talmudic warning against expediting the messianic era, Rabbi Zvi Yehuda responded, "We're not spurring the Redemption—the Redemption is spurring us!" See Rabbi Yosef Bramson, ed., *In the Public Campaign* (Jerusalem, 1985), 24–25 [Hebrew].

8. In the words of Rabbi Yaakov Ariel, "This commandment to settle the Land of Israel within its sacred borders is the primary and perhaps only commandment of many people in this generation through which it might be possible to restore them to faith." Rabbi Yaakov Ariel, "*Torah va'Avodah* in *Bnei Akiva over Time,* Chapter 4: Religious and National Conceptions," in *Fifty Years of Bnei Akiva in Israel,* ed. Mordecai Bar-Lev, Yedidya Cohen, and Shlomo Rosner (Tel Aviv: Bnei Akiva Movement, 1987), 281 [Hebrew].

9. Amos 9:14–15, JPS Tanakh. All quotations from the Bible are from this edition. For more on this view and its roots, see Rabbi Ari

Yitzhak Shvat, "There Shall Not Be Another Exile—On the Sayings of Rabbi Herzog," *Zohar* 21 (2005): 111–122 [Hebrew].

10. Rabbi Zvi Yehuda Kook, *On the Ways of Israel,* Section A, 25, quoted in Ravitzky, *Messianism, Zionism, and Jewish Religious Radicalism,* 173 [Hebrew]. For Rabbi Zvi Yehuda's historiography, see Schwartz, *Challenge and Crisis in Rabbi Kook's Circle,* 38–71 [Hebrew].

11. Rabbi Yaakov Filber, quoted in Ravitzky, *Messianism, Zionism, and Jewish Religious Radicalism,* 183 [Hebrew].

12. The theological interpretation given to this determination by Hanan Porat and his acquaintances does not concern a prediction of the future but the power of human faith to influence the future: "They told me: At the Merkaz HaRav, they believe in 'messianic birth pangs'; they shut their eyes, they can't see reality. I replied: There is innocence, and there is creative innocence, and the fact of innocence is already creative. If it is ever asked, 'Will there be a withdrawal?' complete self-sacrifice will guarantee that this will never, ever happen." Aran, *Kookism,* 6 [Hebrew]. The concept of "creative innocence" was developed in groups associated with the Merkaz, especially by Rabbi Zvi Tau and his wife, Rabbanit Hannah, while other messianic circles, influenced by Kol HaTor, also dealt with forecasting the future and calculating dates when the Messiah might arrive. See Udi Abramovitz, "The State Theology" (Ph.D. diss., Ben-Gurion University of the Negev, 2014), chaps. 1 and 2, and pp. 141–145.

13. Quoted in Ravitzky, *Messianism, Zionism, and Jewish Religious Radicalism,* 184 [Hebrew].

14. The main proponent of this line of faith was Rabbi Mordechai Eliyahu, who made this case, among others, at a prayer rally in Neve Dekalim some two months before the Disengagement. See his comments, for example, on the Arutz 7 website [Hebrew]: http://www .inn.co.il/News/News.aspx/115887. Rabbi Zvi Tau's disciples established the Believe and Sow foundation in Gush Katif, whose job was to ensure "business as usual" and enable farmers to continue sowing their lands for the following year, based on their understanding that "faith determines reality" and so would avert the impending Disengagement.

15. Rabbi Moshe Tzuriel, "Is this really the beginning of the growth of our redemption? Was Rabbi Kook wrong?" From the www.yeshiva .org.il website (accessed January 2006). Tzuriel concludes that despite the various crises, "This is the path of Redemption, and it cannot be otherwise." Rabbi Tzuriel goes on to insist, despite the difficulties, on the messianic interpretation of Zionist history. That said, he hints that the state's leadership was a "rabble" whose origin was not Jewish.

16. For the different reactions to the Disengagement that gained currency within messianic Religious Zionist circles, see Avinoam Rosenak, *Cracks: Unity of Opposites, the Political and Rabbi Kook's Disciples* (Tel Aviv: Riesling, 2013), 137–154 [Hebrew].

17. Rabbi Zvi Tau, *Those Who Hope in the Lord Will Renew Their Strength* [Hebrew].

18. I should note that the vast majority of Religious Zionists were not thrown into a crisis of faith by the Disengagement. That is because faith in the mystical interpretation of secularism and the messianic significance of Zionism never took center stage in the lives of most middle-class Religious Zionists. But the group that *was* flung into a crisis of faith included many of the religious leaders, rabbis, yeshiva heads, and educators of Religious Zionism.

19. All the quotations from opponents of the Disengagement are taken from Rosenak, *Cracks* [Hebrew].

20. Rabbi Kook pointed out and perhaps even predicted this possibility. See "The Process of Ideas in Israel," in *Lights* (*Orot*) (Jerusalem: Rabbi Kook Institute, 1989), 93 [Hebrew].

21. The new left is not so new. It was Yeshayahu Leibowitz who first directed the left's ideological focus toward the occupation, rather than peace, immediately after the Six-Day War. "We have no choice, out of concern for the Jewish people and our state, but to get out of the territories populated by 1.25 million Arabs—without any connection to the question of peace." Leibowitz, "Territories," *Yediot Aharonot,* April–May 1968 [Hebrew]. It took the left forty years to move Leibowitz's exhortation from the movement's margins to its center.

4 A CONFUSING PARADOX

1. The leadership of the Arab League was vigorously opposed to the existence of the Jewish state, and still considers it a foreign organism that refuses to be assimilated into the wider region. See Yuval Arnon-Ohana, *Line of Furrow and Fire: 150 Years of Conflict over the Land of Israel, 1860–2010* (Netanya: Achiasaf, 2013), 157 [Hebrew].

2. For more, see Moshe Yaalon, "Introduction: Restoring a Security-First Peace Policy," in *Israel's Critical Security Requirements for Defensible Borders*, ed. Dan Diker (Jerusalem: Jerusalem Center for Public Affairs, 2010), 7–17.

3. Ibid., 35.

4. I discuss this further in Chapter 6, "No Demographic Problem?"

5. Quoted in Uriel Abulof, *Living on the Edge: The Existential Uncertainty of Zionism* (Haifa: Yediot Books and Haifa University Press, 2015), 2 [Hebrew]. Note, however, that many of Arnon Soffer's predictions—as is the nature of many demographic forecasts—have been proven wrong over the years. Alternative demographic theories will be considered below.

6. One of the most prominent commanders making this suggestion was Yigal Allon. See Udi Manor, *Yigal Allon: Political Biography, 1949–1980* (Or Yehuda: Dvir, 2016), 25–27 [Hebrew].

7. David Ben-Gurion, speech to the Knesset, 4 April 1949, Knesset Protocols, 20th Session of the First Knesset [Hebrew].

8. Amos Oz, "Amos Oz Has a Recipe for Saving Israel," *Haaretz*, 10 March 2015.

5 NO SECURITY PROBLEM?

1. See Uriya Shavit, *The Decline of the West in Muslim-Arab Scholarship* (Tel Aviv: HaKibbutz HaMeuchad, 2010), 15–18 [Hebrew].

2. Note that another trend exists in the Muslim world, one that identifies the disparity in power between the West and Islam as a rallying cry for introspection and change, not for shunning the West. Ibid., 95–110, 142 [Hebrew].

3. Yohanan Tzoref, "Barriers to Resolving the Conflict with Israel: The Palestinian Perspective," in *Barriers to Peace in the Israeli-Palestinian*

Conflict, ed. Yaacov Bar-Siman-Tov (Jerusalem: Jerusalem Institute for Israel Studies, 2010), 58–96. It is worth adding that in the terminology of Islamist groups, such as Hamas and Islamic Jihad, this anti-imperial national resistance is complemented by a religious ideology of holy war against heretics: jihad. As such, many experience this national-religious struggle against Israel as the simultaneous realization of the imperative of muqawama and the commandment of jihad.

4. In recent years, awareness has grown in Israel of a reverse population movement, the creation of an estimated eight hundred thousand Jewish refugees from Arab countries. These Jews were recognized as refugees in Israeli government decisions and in Resolution 185 (2008) of the United States Congress.

5. The precise number of refugees, as well as the circumstances of and reasons for their flight during the war, remain a matter of bitter controversy between Palestinian and Israeli historians, as well as within the Israeli academy. The United Nations Relief and Works Agency (UNRWA), for example, puts the number of refugees at approximately 750,000; see "Palestine Refugees" at https://www.unrwa .org/palestine-refugees.

6. On the role of UNRWA in perpetuating the refugee problem, see Ben-Dror Yemini, *Industry of Lies* (Tel Aviv: Yediot Books, 2014), 92–93 [Hebrew].

7. This definition is according to UNRWA's criteria, in contrast to the definition adopted by the U.N. High Commissioner for Refugees. The 1951 Refugee Convention enshrines the accepted international definition of a refugee, whose criteria the Palestinians do not meet.

8. See Padraig O'Malley, *The Two-State Delusion: Israel and Palestine—A Tale of Two Narratives* (New York: Penguin, 2006), 178. Note that in multiple rounds of negotiations, diplomats have tried to find the right formulation to enable the Palestinians to declare that they have fulfilled their right of return without requiring Israel to absorb a critical mass of refugees. Nevertheless, as one Arab intellectual told me, there exists a discrepancy between the flexibility exhibited by some of the Palestinians in negotiations and the fact that they have never attempted to prepare Palestinian society for such compromises.

9. O'Malley, *The Two-State Delusion,* 48n10.

10. One proposed alternative to the return of the refugees is financial compensation. At the Annapolis Conference, the Palestinians insisted that such compensation should stand at 200 billion dollars, a sum three times larger than Israel's annual budget. Ibid., 196–198.

11. For a good example of how Palestinians would react to such a concession, consider the slip of the tongue of Mahmoud Abbas, president of the Palestinian Authority, in a 2012 interview, when he said that he was prepared to relinquish his personal right to return to his home in Safed. This prompted masses of Palestinians to take to the streets in protest, calling him a traitor. Shortly thereafter, in a further interview, Abbas clarified that no Palestinian leader has the right to cede on behalf of the Palestinian people the right to return to Palestine. That said, a few Palestinian leaders—such as Sari Nusseibeh, a professor of philosophy in Jerusalem and former Palestinian Authority official—exist who take a more moderate tone on the question of return. See Yemini, *Industry of Lies*, 96 [Hebrew].

12. The Palestinians' unwillingness to relinquish the right of return was, according to President Clinton's peace envoy Dennis Ross, the reason for the collapse of the Camp David talks in 2000.

13. The three historical components that attest to the evolution of the belligerent Palestinian mentality can be organized systematically around three dates: 1929, 1947, and 1967. The great violent protest against Zionism as an allegedly colonial movement first erupted in 1929, which is—to quote the title of Hillel Cohen's book—"Year Zero" of the Jewish-Palestinian conflict. The Nakba started in 1947, and the occupation in 1967. Hillel Cohen, *Year Zero of the Arab-Israeli Conflict: 1929* (Waltham, Mass.: Brandeis University Press, 2015).

6 NO DEMOGRAPHIC PROBLEM?

1. See Roberta Seid, Michael L. Wise, and Bennett Zimmerman, "Voodoo Demographics," *Azure* 25 (Summer 2006): 61–78.

2. See Caroline B. Glick, *The Israeli Solution: A One-State Plan for Peace in the Middle East* (New York: Crown Forum, 2014).

3. See Arnon Soffer, *A Decade Since the Establishment of the Team for Denying Palestinian Demographics* (Haifa: Haifa University, 2016) [Hebrew].

4. See Yoram Ettinger, "The Myth of the Arab Demographic Time-Bomb," *NRG.com*, 16 December 2016 [Hebrew].

5. This subject is also controversial. Ettinger argues that the Jewish fertility rate will surpass the Arab fertility rate. Conversely, Soffer argues that the key statistic is not the fertility rate but natural growth—a figure that also accounts for the mortality rate, which is lower among the Palestinians because their population is comparatively young. Therefore, Soffer concludes, natural growth in the Arab population remains higher. Israel Rosner, "The Demographic Demon: How Close Are We to a Binational Reality?" Israel's Channel 10, 27 October 2015, available at: https://www.10.tv/mmnews/132628 [Hebrew].

6. Supporters of annexation justify their proposal by pointing to the results of the annexation of East Jerusalem. The Arabs of East Jerusalem are given Israeli identity cards and certain rights, but they must apply for full citizenship, which would give them the right to vote for the Knesset. To date, most East Jerusalem Arabs have refrained from seeking full Israeli citizenship. Supporters of annexation propose that this result would replicate itself across Judea and Samaria. Just as East Jerusalem was annexed to the State of Israel without making its residents full Israeli citizens, so too the West Bank might be annexed without its residents seeking full Israeli citizenship.

   But such an inference from the present situation in Jerusalem to a future situation in Judea and Samaria is unreasonable. East Jerusalem Arabs refrain from applying for Israeli citizenship because doing so would be taken as recognition of Israel and thereby as a form of treason. If the West Bank Arabs were to apply en masse for Israeli citizenship, millions of Palestinians would be able to vote in Israeli elections, endangering the very existence of Israel as a Jewish state. It is unlikely that an action that would endanger the Jewish character of the State of Israel would be seen as support for such a state.

7. The clearest, most systematic, and most comprehensive formulation of the concept of annexation can be found in Caroline Glick's *The Israeli Solution*. Glick engages throughout with the intellectual challenge presented here. She argues that the absorption of the West

Bank Arabs into Israel would not import brutal violence into Israel but would cause the situation to calm down instead. How so? Glick's argument is based on the premise that the hatred that drives many Palestinians toward violence is largely a result of years of incitement by Palestinian figures, primarily the Palestinian political establishment. This causal link between the Palestinian political establishment and Palestinian hostility toward Israel draws Glick to the conclusion that the breakup of these political institutions would induce this hostility to dissipate. If the West Bank Arabs were absorbed into Israel, they would also be absorbed into its educational system and would no longer be exposed to the cultural and educational systems that nurture and incite violence.

One weakness in Glick's argument, however, is that in the twenty-first century it is difficult to attribute such power over people's consciousness to any political institution. In a world in which incitement goes viral through social media, and in which most of the information to which people are exposed comes not from the education system but from social media, it is difficult to see how disconnecting the Palestinian population from the Palestinian Authority would also detach them from the sources of incitement to violence.

8. Padraig O'Malley, *The Two-State Delusion: Israel and Palestine—A Tale of Two Narratives* (New York: Penguin, 2006), 270.

9. Peter Beinart, "To Save Israel, Boycott the Settlements," *New York Times*, 18 March 2012.

10. The two populations today are subjected, in practice, to two different legal systems. The Palestinians are under military law, while the settlers are covered by civilian law. For an extended discussion, see the detailed report of the Association for Civil Rights in Israel, "One Rule, Two Legal Systems: Israel's Regime of Laws in the West Bank," October 2014, available at https://www.acri.org.il/en/wp-content/uploads/2015/02/Two-Systems-of-Law-English-FINAL.pdf.

11. Dr. Yossi Beilin, an Israeli politician and scholar, quoted in Uriel Abulof, *Living on the Edge: The Existential Uncertainty of Zionism* (Haifa: Yediot Books and Haifa University Press, 2015), 261 [Hebrew].

12. Quoted in Abulof, *Living on the Edge*, 96 [Hebrew].

7 THE MORAL DILEMMA

1. According to Article 49(6) of the Fourth Geneva Convention, it is forbidden for countries to settle their citizens in occupied territory. Nevertheless, the Israeli Supreme Court does not consider the settlements a violation of international law. For a critical analysis of the way in which Supreme Court rulings have legitimized the settlement enterprise, see Talia Sasson, *On the Brink of the Abyss* (Jerusalem: Keter, 2015), 96–137 [Hebrew].

2. See the Association for Civil Rights in Israel, "One Rule, Two Legal Systems: Israel's Regime of Laws in the West Bank," October 2014, available at https://www.acri.org.il/en/wp-content/uploads/2015/02 /Two-Systems-of-Law-English-FINAL.pdf (2014).

3. This discussion, as stated, deals with questions of morality rather than law—indeed, this distinction is by all appearances invalid from the perspective of international law.

4. Yossi Goldstein, *Eshkol: A Biography* (Jerusalem: Keter, 2003), 569–571 [Hebrew].

5. Here too, my distinction is based on moral intuition, not international law.

6. Quoted in Uzi Benziman, "Stop Waiting for the Phone to Ring," *Haaretz*, 22 March 2018, available at https://www.haaretz.com /1.4898615.

7. Politically, the Jordanians relinquished their claim to the West Bank in 1988.

8. I must emphasize that this is an Israeli and Western argument. From an Arab-Muslim perspective, the land was indeed once under independent Muslim rule—that of the Ottoman Empire—but that rule was terminated through British aggression and occupation, which was replaced (as far as Arabs are concerned) by Jewish aggression and occupation. But even in the Arab-Muslim narrative, Ottoman imperial rule is a far cry from Palestinian national rule.

9. See Yitzhak Gal-Nor, "The Territorial Partition of the Land of Israel: The Decision in 1937," *Studies in Israeli and Modern Jewish Society* 1 (1991): 211–240 [Hebrew].

10. One Palestinian justification for the Arabs' rejection of this plan was

that it partitioned the land unfairly: the Jews represented 36 percent of the population but received 56 percent of the territory. See Benny Morris, *1948: A History of the First Arab-Israeli War* (New Haven: Yale University Press, 2008).

11. In fact, both sides accepted the plan with reservations, but Clinton argues in his memoirs that the Israeli reservations fell within his parameters, while the Palestinian reservations fell beyond it. See Bill Clinton, *My Life* (New York: Knopf, 2004), 946–947, 939.

12. This statement—accurately rendered, "the *Arabs* never miss an opportunity to miss an opportunity"—was made on the sidelines of the Geneva Conference with neighboring Arab states on 21 December 1973.

    The academic Elie Podeh disagrees with this accepted narrative. The Palestinians, he argues, have no monopoly on missing opportunities—and the State of Israel has its own history of squandering them. See Podeh, "Israel and the Arab Peace Initiative, 2002–2014: A Plausible Missed Opportunity," *Middle East Journal* 68, no. 4 (2014): 584–603.

13. See Avi Issacharoff, "Peace, Hope, and Recriminations: The Peace Plan That Remained on the Napkin," *Walla News*, 24 May 2013 [Hebrew].

8 THE JEWISH DILEMMA

1. Nachmanides, *Hasagot HaRamban al Sefer HaMitzvot*, Commandment 4 [Hebrew].

2. Maimonides, *Laws of the Sabbath*, 2:3 [Hebrew].

3. Rabbi Ovadia Yosef, *Masa Ovadia* (Jerusalem: Rav Kook Institute, 2007), 331 [Hebrew].

4. Ibid.

5. Rabbi Haim David Halevy, "Peace and Its Consequences," *Oral Torah* 21 (1979): 39–51 [Hebrew].

6. Shaul Tchernichovsky, "Man is nothing but . . ." [Hebrew].

7. Ze'ev Jabotinsky, "Soldiers' Alliance," *Der Moment*, 20 July 1933 [Yiddish].

Yitzhak Shamir expressed this view most forcefully when he said that a withdrawal from the Land of Israel would be "like murdering" Jewish history. Yitzhak Shamir, interview in *Haaretz,* 1 April 1994. See also *Barriers to Peace in the Israeli-Palestinian Conflict,* ed. Yaacov Bar-Siman-Tov (Jerusalem: Jerusalem Institute for Israel Studies, 2010), 197 [Hebrew].

8. David Ben-Gurion, speech at the Twentieth Zionist Congress of August 1937.

9. There would appear to be a contradiction in the Bible's attitude toward residents of the Land of Israel. While the Bible demands great sensitivity toward minorities living in Israel, it also enjoins some harsh violence on residents of the land. I would maintain, however, that the apparent contradiction is false. The Bible displays no tolerance toward the pagan population of the Land of Israel, who might tempt the arriving Hebrews into idolatry. It is the other ethnic minorities, those who do not belong to the seven pagan nations, who are called "foreigners" (*gerim*)—and the great religious test facing the Hebrews is that of showing sensitivity toward *them.*

What does this mean for the Palestinians? Does Jewish law demand that they be treated like the seven Canaanite pagan nations, or are they gerim, in which case sensitivity toward them constitutes the supreme religious test facing the Jews? Maimonides ruled that the Ishmaelites were not pagans but faithful servants of God: "These Ishmaelites are not idol worshippers at all, as idol worship has already been cut off from their mouths and hearts, and they attribute the appropriate singularity to God on High, a singularity without imperfection"; Responsa, 159. In light of this, Rabbi Abraham Isaac Kook determined that not only are the Arabs *not* pagans, they should be seen as resident gerim: "And the main principle is the reason of 'Lo Techonem'—do not grant them residence on your land. Therefore, Ishmaelites are not considered idol worshippers, rather they are resident gerim [strangers], and it is permissible to grant them residence on the land."; Abraham Isaac Kook, *Mishpat Cohen* (Jerusalem: Association for the Publication of Rabbi Kook's Books, 1937) [Hebrew].

10. Theodor Herzl, *Altneuland* (1902), book 3.

9 FROM CONFUSION TO UNDERSTANDING

1. John Stuart Mill, *On Liberty* (1859), chap. 2, available through Project Gutenberg at http://www.gutenberg.org/files/34901/34901-h /34901-h.htm.

2. The Palestinian National Charter. See Yehoshafat Harkabi and Matti Steinberg, *The Palestinian Charter in the Test of Time and Practice* (Jerusalem: Hasbara Center, 1998) [Hebrew].

3. "We should there form a portion of a rampart of Europe against Asia, an outpost of civilization as opposed to barbarism": Theodor Herzl, *The Jewish State* (1896), available from Project Gutenberg at http:// www.gutenberg.org/files/25282/25282-h/25282-h.htm.

4. Let me add a note of personal reservation: I believe that the understanding of Zionism as a colonial movement is mistaken. Zionism lacks some of the most basic characteristics of a classical colonial movement. First and foremost, the Zionists had no motherland sending them to a foreign land to exploit its resources. The British Empire did indeed support Zionism at the close of World War I, but Britain eventually surrendered to Arab pressure and turned its back on Zionism on the eve of World War II, almost totally halting Jewish immigration to Israel. At the end of the day, the Jewish state was created not through the benevolence of the British Empire but through a violent struggle against it. Many Israelis think of themselves as refugees from Europe, or even *orphans* of Europe, but certainly not emissaries *of* Europe.

5. "Hamas Covenant 1988: The Covenant of the Islamic Resistance Movement," 18 August 1988, Article 22, available at http://avalon .law.yale.edu/20th_century/hamas.asp.

6. For a detailed psychological analysis of this feeling of mutual victimhood, see Padraig O'Malley, *The Two-State Delusion: Israel and Palestine —A Tale of Two Narratives* (New York: Penguin, 2006), 47.

7. Prime Minister Tony Blair said this to the British chief rabbi, Lord Jonathan Sacks, who shared the story with members of the Israeli National Library's Global Forum at a conference in December 2016.

8. The event was part of the Jerusalem Sacred Music Festival.

9. Profound theological foundations exist upon which a joint Judeo-Muslim narrative could be built. Religious ideas found in the sphere of Muslim discourse could be synthesized with those found in the sphere of Jewish discourse, forming a new sphere of discourse common to both worlds. Such a synthesis already happened once in the past. The greatest Jewish philosophers, chief among them Maimonides, saw themselves as part of a broad theological conversation conducted in Arabic and engaged in by Muslim thinkers. The synthesis also has firm cultural foundations. Many Israelis are the children and grandchildren of Arabic-speaking Jews who grew up in a Muslim cultural environment. Mizrahi Jews, Buzaglo told me, could well pave the way toward a new Judeo-Muslim narrative. If the twentieth century produced such philosophers as Rabbi Abraham Joshua Heschel, who emphasized the common heritage and destiny of Christianity and Judaism, could the twenty-first century likewise produce philosophers capable of expressing the common heritage and destiny of Judaism and Islam?

10. Rabbi Froman's words were recounted by one of his students, the poet Eliaz Cohen, to me.

11. Babylonian Talmud, Chagigah 3b, trans. Adin Steinsaltz, in the William Davidson Talmud, Sefaria Library, Sefaria.org.

12. Ibid.

PART III INTRODUCTION

1. See Israel Kolatt, "Religion, Society, and State During the Period of the National Home," in *Zionism and Religion,* ed. Shmuel Almog, Jehuda Reinharz, and Anita Shapira (Hanover, N.H.: Brandeis University Press in association with the Zalman Shazar Center for Jewish History, University Press of New England, 1998), 366.

2. For more on Ben-Gurion's principle of mamlachtiyut, see Natan Yanai, "Ben Gurion's Concept of *Mamlachtiyut,*" *Cathedra* 45 (September 1987): 169–189 [Hebrew].

3. Menachem Ussishkin, speech to the 20th Zionist Congress (1937): *Protocols of the Third Meeting of the Twentieth Zionist Congress and the Fifth*

Session of the Jewish Agency Council, Zurich, 3–21 August 1937, Steno-graphic Report (Jerusalem: World Zionist Organization and Jewish Agency, 1937), 38 [Hebrew].

4. Ben-Gurion's ideological partner Berl Katznelson died before the establishment of the state, but he was the figure who led the labor movement from a hardline ideological position toward a softer, more dynamic way of thinking. Katznelson believed that ideas should shape reality but should also be permitted to *be shaped* by reality. I label such an outlook "pragmatic."

   But some disagree. The Israeli writer Assaf Inbari, for example, argues that Berl Katznelson ought not to be viewed as a pragmatist. In an enlightening essay, Inbari demonstrates that Katznelson's path should be viewed as a movement rather than an example of pragma-tism. Pragmatism, he argues, means compromising on one's values— while a movement *realizes* values. The difference is that movements aim to realize values that are already dynamic, rather than rigid, and befit a dynamic reality. See Assaf Inbari, "Berl's Option," *Panim* (August 2001) [Hebrew], available on Assaf Inbari's website: http://inbari.co.il/#content-articles.

10 THE PARTIAL-PEACE PLAN

1. The plan was first presented on 29 July 1967. See the website of the Yigal Allon Center (bet-alon.co.il), as well as Anita Shapira, *Yigal Allon, Native Son: A Biography,* trans. Evelyn Abel (Philadelphia: University of Pennsylvania Press, 2008).

2. This area is delineated by the Jordanian border in the east, the Allon Road in the West, Nahal Bezek in the north, and the northern area of the Dead Sea in the south. See Lee Cahaner, Arnon Sofer, and Yuval Kna'an, *The Future of the Jordan Valley: Keeping It Under Israeli Sover-eignty, Pros and Cons* (Haifa: Haifa University Press, 2006), 9 [Hebrew].

3. Many are familiar with the Allon Plan from the map of Israel's pro-posed new borders; see, e.g., Martin Gilbert, *The Routledge Atlas of the Israeli Arab Conflict,* 10th ed. (London: Routledge, 2012), 137. But Yigal Allon preferred to avoid drawing maps. He understood the plan more as a general conception than as a specific map, and one

that should remain dynamic and adaptable in light of changes. See Udi Manor, *Yigal Allon: Political Biography, 1949–1980* (Or Yehuda: Dvir, 2016), 276 [Hebrew].

4. One weakness in this argument is that in the present reality, in which knowledge and technological know-how are easily transferable over the internet, the residents of Judea and Samaria could find out how to manufacture weapons by themselves. Thus an Israeli presence in the Jordan Valley and at its crossing points would be insufficient: in order to guarantee the complete demilitarization of the territories, the Israeli army would have to retain a presence across the entire area. Such a case was presented to me by several senior military figures. I also heard the contrary argument, however: that the relative calm since 2004 (as of the end of 2016) is the product not so much of Israel's military presence in Judea and Samaria but rather mostly of the efforts of the Palestinian Authority and its coordination with Israel. The same military figures emphasized that the perpetuation of the status quo actually endangers this vital security coordination.

   As previously stated, I distinguish between two kinds of dangers: security dangers and existential dangers. Here I elaborate upon this distinction. The danger involved in withdrawing from the Jordan Valley is different from the one involved in withdrawing from the rest of the territories. Whereas a withdrawal from other parts of the territories would constitute a security danger, a withdrawal from the Jordan Valley specifically would constitute an existential danger. The Partial-Peace Plan is intended to safeguard Israel from the existential demographic threat without converting that threat into yet another existential threat. As such, even though the plan is not free of security dangers, it will at least liberate Israel from its existential trap.

5. It would probably be necessary to create territorial corridors connecting the demilitarized Palestinian state and the Kingdom of Jordan. These corridors would traverse the buffer zone formed by the Jordan Valley between Jordan and Palestine, and would constitute the primary entry and exit points into and out of Palestine. These crossings could be supervised, but they would still have to allow for traffic to flow and breathe.

6. See Khaled Abu Toameh, "The Secret Ethnic Cleansing of Palestinians," Gatestone Institute, 10 August 2015. Amnon Lord's analysis is
also interesting in this regard: Amnon Lord, "Abu Mazen Sacrifices
18,000 Refugees in the Name of the Palestinian Right of Return,"
Mida, 26 May 2015 [Hebrew].

7. One of the greatest strategic flaws in proposals for a permanent accord is that the Jordan Valley would not remain under Israel's long-
term control. In Bill Clinton's parameters for a final-status accord, for
example, the IDF would guard certain military outposts in the Jordan
Valley for six years, whereupon it would have to withdraw. Other
plans speak of the long-term presence of international troops alone.
The experience of several rounds of negotiations teaches that no
comprehensive peace agreement is possible if the Jordan Valley remains in Israeli hands. But any accord that does *not* leave the Jordan
Valley in Israeli hands would be an accord that does not leave Israel's
security in its own hands either.

   If we compare the left's dream of a final-status accord to the annexation plan envisaged by sections of the right, we can see that they
are mirror images of each other. Just as the annexation of Judea and
Samaria would cause Israel's demographic collapse, a full withdrawal
from Judea and Samaria would cause Palestine's demographic collapse as well because of the influx of refugees. A partial withdrawal,
however, would avert these twin demographic dangers.

8. Note that Israel's security needs encompass more than the Jordan
Valley. Israel has additional needs, which translate into defense
arrangements that are vital for guaranteeing Israel's security. These
include Israel's continued control of the electromagnetic spectrum,
airspace, and certain areas adjacent to the Green Line and in the
vicinity of Ben Gurion Airport. All such arrangements would violate
Palestinian sovereignty, and so could be achieved only if Israel relinquished its demand for an end of claims from the Palestinians. See
the articles by Uzi Dayan, Giora Eiland, and Aharon Ze'evi Farkash,
in *Israel's Critical Security Requirements for Defensible Borders*, ed. Dan
Diker (Jerusalem: Jerusalem Center for Public Affairs, 2010).

9. In contrast, there exists a detailed security paradigm that says it

is possible to achieve existential security even through a comprehensive withdrawal within the framework of a permanent accord. Security would be achieved through special security arrangements. This position was articulated well by Shaul Arieli. See Shaul Arieli, *A Border Between Us and You: The Israeli-Palestinian Conflict and Ways to Its Resolution* (Tel Aviv: Aliyat Hagag Books, Yediot Aharonot, 2013) [Hebrew]. While I disagree with Arieli for the various reasons presented throughout this book, his position is important and challenging.

10. The argument I make in this book might not be too far from Allon's original intentions. According to one biographer, Yigal Allon did not regard his own plan as a permanent solution at all, but as a temporary and partial plan that could pave the way to a permanent political accord. See Manor, *Yigal Allon*, 280 [Hebrew].

11. The Jordan Valley covers roughly one quarter of the area of Judea and Samaria, but this fact does not necessarily determine Israel's security needs. It is perfectly possible that the same degree of security could be achieved through an even more extensive withdrawal from the Jordan Valley, because the valley's importance for Israel's security has changed over the years. In Yigal Allon's day, the Jordan Valley served as a physical buffer blocking an invasion by a hostile army, whereas today its primary importance lies in preventing the movement of weapons and people.

The change in the Jordan Valley's security function affects the size of the area that Israel would need to retain. If the Jordan Valley is no longer intended to serve as a deployment base for armored brigades and infantry, but rather to function as a buffer to prevent the movement of weapons and people, then Israel no longer needs to continue controlling the entire area. According to some security experts, it would be enough to hold a two kilometer (1.2 mile)–wide strip between Route 90 and the Jordan River. See Ilan Goldenberg, Gadi Shamni, Nimrod Novik, and Kris Bauman, *Advancing the Dialogue: A Security System for the Two-State Solution* (Washington, D.C.: Center for a New American Security, 2016).

The settlement blocs cover some 5 percent of Judea and Samaria. These include the Maale Adumim bloc, Gush Etzion, most of the Jewish neighborhoods of East Jerusalem, the Ariel bloc, the Hashmonaim bloc, the Shaked bloc, Alfei Menashe, and others. Add Kiryat Arba and the Jewish settlement in Hebron, and the amount increases to some 6–7 percent. See Shaul Arieli, *People and Borders*, 2nd ed. (Israel, 2011), 275, available at http://www.shaularieli.com /image/users/77951/ftp/my_files/articles_in_english/people_and_bor dersNEW.pdf?id=7934192. The settlement blocs are defined in accordance with Netanyahu's use of the term as analyzed in Shaul Arieli, "West Bank Settlement Blocs Blocking Israel's Progress Towards Stability," *Haaretz,* 14 March 2016, available at https://www.haaretz .com/israel-news/.premium-settlement-blocs-blocking-progress -toward-stability-1.5416599).

The importance of defensible borders is understood in the common American interpretation of U.N. Security Council Resolution 242. See Dore Gold, "Regional Overview: How Defensible Borders Remain Vital for Israel," in *Israel's Critical Security Requirements for Defensible Borders*, 19–33.

12. The Middle East scholar Fouad Ajami phrased it thus: "Memory stood in the way of accommodation. An apparition, the Old Palestine rebuked this practical peace. Memory sanctified all that had been there before the loss and the defeat." Fouad Ajami, *The Dream Palace of the Arabs* (New York: Vintage, 1999), 270.

13. Muslims traditionally divide the world into two areas: the House of Islam (*Dar al-Islam*), the lands under Muslim sovereignty, in which Muslims can live in security, and the House of War (*Dar al-Harb*), comprising the lands under the rule of heretics, in which Muslims cannot live in peace. Under Islamic law, the Muslim faithful are enjoined to convert territories of Dar al-Harb into areas of Dar al-Islam, and this prescription applies even more strongly to lands that were once under the Dar al-Islam. For further elaboration, see Bernard Lewis, *The Crisis of Islam* (London: Weidenfeld and Nicolson, 2003).

Additionally, Hamas and similar Islamist movements have defined the entire Land of Israel as *waqf*. Waqf is a legal category that originally referred to lands endowed for the social and religious needs of the public—land allocated for mosques, cemeteries, schools, and so forth. This classification imposes certain restrictions on the sale, purchase, taxation, and inheritance of such lands that do not apply to other types of land. The application of this category to the entire Land of Israel carries with it symbolic connotations of sanctification, which in turn entail practical connotations under Islamic law for any possibility of negotiating over that land.

14. Palestinian intellectuals told me in private that they are not personally concerned by the matter of Islamic law, but they are aware that such sensitivities form part of the conscience of many of their fellow Palestinians.

15. This was also Henry Kissinger's analysis of the failure to reach a peace deal between Israel and the Palestinians. The Americans' and Israelis' insistence that the Palestinians renounce their claims is precisely what put off the Arab side. See Itamar Rabinovich, *The Lingering Conflict: Israel, the Arabs, and the Middle East, 1948–2012* (Washington, D.C.: Brookings Institution Press, 2012).

16. See Yitzhak Reiter, "Religion as a Barrier to Compromise in the Israeli-Palestinian Conflict," in *Barriers to Peace in the Israeli-Palestinian Conflict,* ed. Yaacov Bar-Siman-Tov (Jerusalem: Jerusalem Institute for Israel Studies, 2010), 228–265. The former Mossad chief Efraim Halevy has said that Hamas once offered Israel a hudna: see "Efraim Halevy: In 1997, Yassin Offered a 30-Year Hudna," *Ynet,* 23 March 2004 [Hebrew]. And we must not rule out the possibility that the Palestinians might eventually experience the sort of identity transformation that would enable them to sign a comprehensive peace deal with Israel.

17. On the eve of the Camp David talks, Yasser Arafat clarified for the Israeli and American negotiations that he could under no circumstances sign a document that would end Palestinian claims toward Israel. See Hirsh Goodman, *The Anatomy of Israel's Survival* (New York: Public Affairs Books, 2011), 76–77. Arafat's remarks aptly present and elucidate the Palestinian trap. Declaring a final end to the conflict would mean changing the ethos of the Palestinian struggle.

18. See the concluding chapter ("The New World Order Reconsidered") of Henry Kissinger, *Diplomacy* (London: Simon and Schuster, 1994).

19. In March 2002, the Arab League adopted the Saudi initiative for

ending the Israeli-Palestinian conflict, which would in turn end the conflict between Israel and the Arab world. The document stipulates that besides a withdrawal to the lines of 4 June 1967, there must also be a "just and agreed" solution to the refugee problem in accordance with Resolution 194 of the U.N. General Assembly. The phrase "just and agreed" is vague and open to multiple interpretations, but the final communiqué of the 2002 summit noted that the Arab League rejected any potential solution that would involve resettling the refugees away from their original homes in what is now Israel. It seems that the Saudis have yet to cross the Rubicon, and have not explicitly forgone the return of the refugees in exchange for a territorial withdrawal. The Partial-Peace Plan would allow for the realization of the Saudi interest in ending the occupation, without forgoing the right of return and without requiring the Saudis to fully recognize Israel.

20. There is one difficult, complex problem that the Partial-Peace Plan will also have to confront: the future of the settlements in Judea and Samaria. What follows is a possible way of dealing with the challenge of the settlements within the framework of a partial agreement. A partial withdrawal from the territories would leave the vast majority of the settlements and settlers under Israeli control. The problem is that numerous settlements, containing thousands of people, would remain in the areas from which Israel would withdraw.

There is no substantive reason why these settlements should be evacuated. If the State of Israel contains an Arab minority, why should there not be a Jewish minority in the State of Palestine? That said, this position is problematic, because a withdrawal would still seriously harm the population left behind. It might not remove them from their homes, but it would remove them from their country. For that reason, as part of the Partial-Peace Plan, a solution must be found for the basic security needs of the Jewish population that would remain on the sovereign soil of Palestine.

Researchers at the Institute for National Security Studies (INSS) have proposed a creative and complex framework that might achieve this. Their idea is to carve out very small spaces for partial Jewish autonomy inside the State of Palestine. These special areas would have their own security arrangements. The idea was outlined in 2013 by Professor Gideon Biger and former Ehud Barak adviser Gilead Sher; for a description of the plan, see Gilead Sher, *The Battle for Home* (Tel Aviv: Yediot Books, 2016), 150–154 [Hebrew]. While Sher expresses skepticism about his own plan, we should still treat it with great seriousness and explore how it might be implemented.

Any plan to translate this interesting idea into reality will need to include a series of vital security components, such as the settlements' capacity for self-defense, technological supervision by the IDF to alert settlers in case of danger, and the right for Israel to militarily intervene to defend the settlements in case of attack. This will require special arrangements for the roads that connect the settlements to sovereign Israel. This plan will certainly sound improbable at first hearing, and it is indeed convoluted and complicated, but if Israel could work out how to implement it, Israel could withdraw from the territories without evacuating the settlers but without abandoning them either.

In other words, the Partial-Peace Plan requires the examination of two different types of security arrangements: those that protect the State of Israel from Palestine and those that protect the Jewish settlements inside Palestine. Just as great creativity is needed for security arrangements facing a Palestinian state, equal creativity is required for the security arrangements to protect the settlements remaining inside the Palestinian state. This is undoubtedly an extremely complicated plan, but the problem is also complicated and needs to be tackled with equal complexity.

The proposed security arrangements would be extremely difficult for the Palestinians to accept. The necessary arrangements to protect the settlers remaining in sovereign Palestinian territory would be an affront to Palestinian sovereignty, and the State of Israel would have to offer appropriate compensation. I can suggest one idea for consideration: a one-for-one trade—for every Jew remaining in Palestine, the State of Israel would absorb one Palestinian refugee within its own sovereign borders. This "settlers for refugees" formula would not undermine Israel's demography. The State of Israel can absorb several tens of thousands of refugees without undermining its Jewish majority. The rationale behind this idea is straightforward: the mass evacuation of tens of thousands of settlers is likely to tear Israeli society apart, while absorbing tens of thousands of Palestinians might be problematic but would neither destroy Israeli society nor rupture its delicate social fabric.

11 THE DIVERGENCE PLAN

1. Jeffrey Goldberg, "World Chaos and World Order: Conversations with Henry Kissinger," *Atlantic,* 10 November 2016.

2. Nobody knows for certain how many Palestinians live in Area C, and estimates differ wildly. The lower estimate, as claimed by the Jewish Home Party leader Naftali Bennett in 2012, is fifty thousand. The IDF's Coordinator of Government Activities in the Territories said the same year that there were ninety thousand. The upper estimate is three hundred thousand, the figure proposed by the United Nations Office for the Coordination of Humanitarian Aid (OCHA) in 2017. The dispute is partly derived from disagreement over which localities should be counted as part of Area C, because many Palestinian homes there are "overspill" from Area B rather than self-contained villages.

3. The Divergence Plan can be understood as a pragmatic variation on the Roadmap for peace proposed by the Quartet (the United Nations, the United States, the European Union, and Russia) in 2002 and finalized in 2003, which became the flagship initiative of the George W. Bush administration. That said, one of the major differences between plans is that the Roadmap proposed the establishment of a Palestinian state on temporary borders, with which Israel would negotiate a permanent accord; but the Divergence Plan proposes the establishment of a Palestinian state without any commitment by the Palestinians to work toward an end to their claims, and without any Israeli commitment to withdrawing from the remaining territory. The pragmatic shift in thinking means abandoning the vision of a permanent accord in a region that contains everything but permanence.

4. This idea appears as Phase II of the 2003 Roadmap.

5. An additional adjustment would be needed: non-recognition of the borders of Palestine. In other words, Israel would recognize Palestine but not its borders. By undertaking this, Israel could enhance the Palestinians' independence without complicating matters for Israeli settlers and soldiers.

    The model that could be applied for Palestine is the model of the State of Israel itself. Israel is a member of the international community, but the other 192 member states of the United Nations do not recognize its precise borders. Israel could push for a diplomatic effort to recognize a Palestine without recognized borders, just like Israel. The formula is: two states with unrecognized borders for two peoples.

6. Both left and right are debating various plans to transfer Arab neighborhoods of East Jerusalem to the Palestinian Authority outside the framework of a comprehensive political accord. At one end is the Peace and Security Association plan, presented by the former vice prime minister Haim Ramon, for a unilateral withdrawal from certain Arab sectors of Jerusalem; and on the other end is a more moderate plan advanced by the military historian and journalist Yoaz Hendel for Israel to disengage from the Arab neighborhoods behind the Security Barrier, which intersects parts of East Jerusalem.

7. Professor Robert Aumann presented such an idea in an interview published in *Makor Rishon,* 9 June 2016, that was part of a series of articles by Sarah Haetzni-Cohen. Israeli hi-tech professionals who had heard of this idea described to me innovative technologies that could help advance transport contiguity without territorial contiguity. "The Startup Nation can devise technological solutions for political problems," said one.

8. Other ideas in circulation among experts could be implemented as part of the territorial effort. For example, the supervised traffic at crossings between Palestine and Jordan could be eased, perhaps even through the addition of a purpose-built Palestinian terminal at Amman Airport, such that the Palestinian Authority would enjoy not only territorial contiguity but also a gateway to the world.

9. There are other alternatives that could create a separation at a low cost. In his book *The Battle for Home,* for example, Gilead Sher pro-

poses a series of steps that could entrench the separation between the two political entities without assuming further security risks, including reducing the visible presence of the IDF in the territories, minimizing the involvement of the Civil Administration, improving the economic situation by enhancing freedom of movement, and more. Sher, *The Battle for Home* (Tel Aviv: Yediot Books, 2016), 202–217 [Hebrew].

10. I add a reservation to this plan: What would happen if it turned out that in order to create Palestinian transport contiguity between the various areas under P.A. control, Israel would have to evacuate a number of outposts or settlements? This dilemma might not arise, but whether it did would depend on the professional assessment of the experts who would plan the road network to link up the P.A. areas. I raise this potential dilemma in order to illustrate that the plan described above is a generalized framework only, and it leaves room for continued pragmatic debate within Israeli society.

11. Yehoshua, interview with Razi Barkai on Army Radio, 19 January 2016.

12. There is a certain similarity between Yehoshua's idea and Naftali Bennett's Tranquilization Plan, but there is also a substantial difference between them. Bennett proposes to grant rights to the Palestinians who live in Area C as part of annexing that territory, while Yehoshua emphasizes that he does not propose annexing the Jewish settlements but only granting rights to the Palestinian residents of the area. In the internal logic of the Divergence Plan presented above, Area C would be shrunk and sections would be attached to the Palestinian Authority, in order to facilitate transport contiguity and the growth of Palestinian villages and towns. The proposal to annex Area C to the State of Israel is rooted, it seems, in ideological motives, and it does not serve to extricate Israel from its Catch-67.

12 POLITICAL PRAGMATISM AS A BRIDGE BETWEEN THE LEFT AND THE RIGHT

1. The traditional ideological solutions—annexation versus a peace accord—have been joined in recent years by a surprising new ideo-

logical plan: two states, one homeland. Whereas the annexation plan effectively abandons the realization of the vision of peace, and the two-state solution effectively abandons the vision of settlement, "Two States, One Homeland" seeks to fulfill both dreams at the same time. This plan is the opposite of a pragmatic plan, containing the assumption that in this Middle Eastern struggle of identities the most realistic solution is not to relinquish any dreams but to realize them all simultaneously. Details can be found on the website of Two States, One Homeland: http://2states1homeland.org (English: http://www.alandforall.org/english-main).

2. The Divergence Plan leaves the IDF's military presence in place; as such, it entails fewer security risks than the Partial-Peace Plan, but it does little to reduce the "occupation."

AFTERWORD

1. To some degree, we can distinguish between the revolutionary pioneers of the Zionist movement and the pragmatic founders of the Jewish state. The success of Zionism derives in part from the combination of these two forces.

2. See the World Bank figures for 2017 available at https://data.worldbank.org/indicator/NY.GDP.PCAP.CD?view=map (accessed on 17 March 2018).

ACKNOWLEDGMENTS

This exemplary translation of *Catch-67* is the work of Eylon Levy. Thanks to his cultural adaptability and rich vocabulary, he was able to translate from Hebrew to English not only the substance of the original language but also its energy, and I thank him from the bottom of my heart. I am very grateful to Amy Klein, Leah Beinhaker, and Ben Reis for their contributions to the translation process. I thank my good friend Boaz Lifschitz for his support, faith, and friendship; this book would not have been published in English without him.

Israel's political discourse is based not only on a clash between left and right; there is also a dispute no less seething between religious and secular. This book is the first of two that will explore the intellectual roots of modern Israeli identity. I have offered a philosophical take on the political dispute between left and right; my next book will follow up with a philosophical analysis of both religious and secular identities and of the clash between the two. Together, the two books will explore the hidden ideas underlying Israel's fractured national conversation. I am indebted to the editor of these books, Shmuel Rosner, for the years of our joint exploration of the hidden recesses of modern Israeli identity.

The various discussions in this book were blessed to benefit from the plentiful advice, ideas, corrections, and suggestions of a great many friends. Many thanks to Avishai Ben Sasson, Udi Avramovich, Udi Manor, Itai Heimlich, Eli Ben Meir, Eliran Zered, Efrat Shapira Rosenberg, Assaf Granot, Ariel Horowitz, Ariel Steinberg, Boaz Lifschitz, Ben Avrahami, Batya Huri, Guy Eisenkot, Dudi Feuchtwanger, Rabbi Gavi Goldman, Jonny Clar, Gilad Fulman, Yivniyah Kaploun, Yuval Kahan, Yonatan Nevo, Yitzhak Mor, Yishai Peleg, Israel Rosner, Micah Issolson, Malka Elimelech, Noam Gesundheit, Noam Zion, Sallai Meridor, Samuel Boumendil, Regev Ben David, Rani Alon, Rotem Reichman, Shlomi Pasternak, Sarah Fuchs, and Tamar Ettinger. I owe a special thanks to Ariel Steinberg and Rabbi Danny Segal for their great contribution to the development of this book.

Several figures in the Israeli security and intelligence communities and in the Palestinian cultural and intellectual worlds expanded my horizons and helped me clarify my thoughts. They asked not to be mentioned by name, but I thank them anonymously for their great contribution.

I thank Alon Naveh, my dedicated research assistant for this project, for his meticulous work. And I thank Chaya Eckstein, Imri Zertal, and the whole team at Kinneret Zmora–Bitan Dvir for their thorough and professional work.

This book could not have been written without the great intellectual climate in the place it was written: the Shalom Hartman Institute in Jerusalem. I thank the president of the Hartman Institute, Donniel Hartman, from the bottom of my heart, as well as Yehuda Kurtzer and the whole Hartman team in Israel and the

United States for their support and faith, which made the writing of this book possible.

I wish to thank Haviv Rettig Gur and the agents who represented me faithfully, Peter and Amy Bernstein, for the connections they made that forged the way for this book's publication in the United States. I wish to thank Bill Nelson for the cartography and the staff at Yale University Press, especially Heather Gold and Susan Laity, for their professional work and the serious thought they invested in improving the original manuscript and adapting it for an English-speaking readership.

The thoughts laid out in this book were developed over many years of researching the philosophies that, whether openly or clandestinely, are fueling the dispute between Jews in Israel. My deepest thanks to the team behind Beit Midrash Yisraeli–Ein Prat, led by Anat Silverstone, for our collective journey into the depths of Israel's divisions, and for their efforts every single day to build an academy and a community of people who are kind to one another, who know how to listen, and who work together to heal the fissures in Israeli society.

INDEX

Page numbers in bold indicate maps.

Dayan, Moshe, 21, 37–38, 100, 196n9
debate: "catch" in, 138–140, 146; decline of political debate, x–xi; emotional traps in, 7–14; identity politics in, 120–122; in Talmud, 5–7, 14, 127–129, 177–178
democracy, 57, 70, 87–88, 187n17
demographics: after Six-Day War, 32–33, 193n30; forecasts of natural growth, 84, 207n5; growth rate of Arab population, 34, 207n5; of Jews in Israel, 27–28, 32–35, 69–71, 82–87, 139–140, 160–161, 207n5, 220n20; of Palestinians, 32–34, 75–76, 82–85, 205nn5,7, 222n2; security and, 32–34, 69–73, 82–84, 86–87, 138, 193n30, 220n20
Disengagement Plan, 33, 57–60, 118–119, 202n14
Divergence Plan, 141, 156–159, 163–164, 168, 222nn2,3, 224n12, 225n2
Don-Yehiya, Eliezer, 182n2

East Jerusalem, 99, 158, 207n5, 223n6
Eban, Abba, 103
Egypt, **xiv**; agreement for partial withdrawal by Israel, 147; Camp David Accords, 47–48, 103, 146–147, 192n26,

198n16, 219n17; peace negotiations with Israel, 43–45, 192n26, 195n4; in Six-Day War, 43, 99; United Arab Republic, 1; Yom Kippur War, 43, 196n9
Eldad, Israel, 33, 34
Eliyahu, Mordechai, 202n14
emotional barriers in Israeli-Palestinian conflict, 7–12, 38, 74–79, 148, 204nn2,3, 205n8, 206nn11,12, 218n12
Eshkol, Levi, 99
Ettinger, Yoram, 83–84, 86, 207n5
evacuations of settlements, 56–57, 109, 202n12, 220n20, 224n10

fear in Jewish history, 7–10, 24, 38, 98, 180n10, 183nn2,3, 184n4
Filber, Yaakov, 56
First Aliyah, 55
First Intifada (1987), 32, 46–47, 199n18
Froman, Menachem, 126

Gahlat (Pioneering Torah Scholar Group), 200n3
Gaza Strip, **xiv,** 1, 33, 57, 118–119, 195n42
Glick, Caroline, 207n7
Golan Heights, 1, 43
Greater Israel, 4, 29–32, 46, 52, 70–71, 120, 192n24
Greenberg, Uri Zvi, 33

Green Line, 144, 152, 215n4, 219n19
Gush Katif, 57, 202n14

HaLevi, Hayim David, 109–110
Halevy, Efraim, 219n16
Hamas, 122–123, 204n3, 218n13
haqq al-'awda (right of return), 76–79, 148, 205n8, 206n11
Hashomer Hatzair, 196n9
Hazan, Yaakov, 196n9
Hebrew language, 171–172
Hendel, Yoaz, 223n6
Herzl, Theodor, 116, 171, 182n1, 189n20, 190n21
Heschel, Abraham Joshua, 213n9
hudna, 149–150, 219n16
humiliation: in Palestinian historical consciousness, 9–12, 74–79, 148, 180n14, 205n8; rise of the West, 10–11, 74–75, 204nn2,3; trauma of 1948 war, 148, 218n12
Hussein ibn Talal (King of Jordan), 99, 100–101

IDF (Israel Defense Forces): impact of service on soldiers, 32, 98; Jewish security in State of Palestine, 220n20; in Jordan Valley, 143–145, 216n7, 217n11; Lebanon War, 197n11; military administration in territories, 8–9, 96–97, 108–109; War of Independ-ence, 41, 70–72, 75–78, 148, 205n8, 218n12; Yom Kippur War, 43, 196n9. *See also* Six-Day War

Inbari, Assaf, 214n4
individual liberalism (Jabotinsky), 33, 59
INSS (Institute for National Security Studies), 220n20
intifadas, 2, 32, 46–48, 103, 198n17, 199n18
Irgun, 31, 190n21
Ish-Shalom, Benjamin, 200n3
Islam: ceasefire agreements in Islamic law (*hudna*), 149–150, 219n16; common heritage with Judaism, 125–127, 213n9; jihad in, 204n3; legit-imacy of Jewish sovereignty, 148–150, 218n13, 219n14; religious embarrassment within, 10–12, 180n14; and Western civilization, 3, 10–11, 74–75, 78, 180n14, 204nn2,3
Israel, State of, **xiv**; absorption of Palestinian refugees, 220n20; annexation as risk of desta-bilization, 82–85, 207nn5,6, 216n7; Arab population in, 84–85; Camp David summit, 47–48, 103, 198n16, 219n17; civil rights in, 160–161, 208n10; as democracy, 70, 87, 97–98; demographics of, 32–34, 60, 69–72, 82–85,

193n30, 207n5; diplomatic recognition of Palestinian state, 223n5; escaping the "catch," 138–140, 147; Jewish identity of, 70–72, 82–86, 89, 207n5; on a Jewish majority in, 27–28, 32–35, 70–71, 83–87, 139–140, 160–161, 207n5, 220n20; legal system, 30, 71, 87–88, 208n10, 209n1; moral conviction in, 174; occupation policies, 94–95; Palestinian recognition of, 89; peace initiatives of, 43–45, 196n8, 196n9; return of territories after Six-Day War, 100; secular character of, 134–135; socialism in, 40–42, 135–136; strength of, 173–174; War of Independence, 41, 70–72, 75–78, 148, 205n8, 218n12. *See also* Ben-Gurion, David; Six-Day War

Israel Defense Forces. *See* IDF

Israeli-Palestinian conflict: "catch" in, 138–140, 147; emotional barriers in, 7–12, 38, 74–79, 148, 204nn2,3, 205n8, 206nn11,12, 218n12; psychological aspects of, 7–12, 31–32, 38, 74–79, 148, 204nn2,3, 218n12; Saudi initiatives, 219n19

Israelis: birthrates, 82, 207n5; on the demographic problem, 32–33, 69–70, 73, 82–83, 193n30; fear felt by, 7–10, 32–33, 38, 69–70, 180n10, 193n30; historical memory, 10, 24, 71, 91–92, 180n10, 184n4; on Palestinian refugees' right of return (*haqq al-ʿawda*), 76–78, 205n8; Palestinians perceived by, 7, 8–11, 199n18; social awareness of, 42, 119–122

Jabotinsky, Ze'ev: on Arabs, 23–28, 184n4; Begin as successor to, 30–31, 44, 190n21, 192nn23,24,26; on British Mandate, 23–24, 183n1; on democracy, 187n17; on the individual, 26–27, 33, 59, 186n15, 191n22; on a Jewish majority in Israel, 34–35, 187n17, 194nn37,39; on Jewish migration to Palestine, 24–25, 34–35; Judaism in life of, 20, 182n3, 189n20; on militarism, 26, 190n21, 195n41; nationalism of, 27–29, 112, 186n15; political philosophy of, 26–28, 33; territorial maximalism of, 28–29, 33–34, 59, 194n36; on universal suffrage, 27–28, 34–35, 187n17; Zionist movement criticized by, 23–24, 28–29, 183n2, 185n6

196n9; settlement of, 54–55, 107–109, 114–116, 192n26, 201n8, 211n9; as *waqf,* 218n13, 219n14

Law of Return (Israel), 84

Lebanon, **xiv,** 197n11

left, Israeli: after Six-Day War, 21; on Arab demographics, 83; Cold War's impact on, 41; defined, 4; ideological shifts in, 46, 60–61, 198n13, 203n21; Meretz Party, 196n6; new left, 60–61, 203n21; on occupation, 98, 104; on peace process, 20–21, 37–40, 167–168, 195n1, 196n6; Second Intifada's impact on, 47–48, 103, 198nn17,18; on security, 73–74, 89, 90–91, 98; social agenda of, 20–21; and two-state solution, 82; Western sensibility of, 91, 92; on withdrawal, 89–91, 117. *See also* Partial-Peace Plan

Lehi, 31, 190n21, 195n41

Leibowitz, Yeshayahu, 193n30, 196n9, 203n21

Livni, Tzipi, 31, 33, 34

Madrid Conference (1991), 45

Maimonides, 10, 106, 211n9, 213n9

mamlachtiyut, 135

Mapai (Workers Party), 30, 37–38, 135

Mapam, 196n6

Marx, Karl, 38–39

Meir, Golda, 21, 38

Melamed, Zalman, 59

Meretz Party, 196n6

Meridor, Dan, 31, 34

Merkaz HaRav Yeshiva, 200n3, 202n12

messianism: creative innocence, 202nn12,14; of Abraham Isaac Kook, 51; liberalism, 35, 40, 46; reactions of messianics to Disengagement Plan, 57–58, 202nn12,14, 203n15; Redemption, 52, 54–59, 203nn15,18; Religious Zionism, 51–52; Six-Day War, 52, 182n2. *See also* Kook, Zvi Yehuda

Mill, John Stuart, 120

moral aspects of occupation, 78–79, 93–94, 98–100, 113–116

Movement for Civil Rights and Peace (Ratz), 196n6

muqawama, 74, 204n3

Muslims: common heritage with Judaism, 125–127, 213n9; humiliation felt by, 10–12, 180n14; legitimacy of Jewish sovereignty, 148–150, 209n8, 218n13, 219n14; religious embarrassment among, 10–12, 180n14; worldview of, 218n13

mysticism, 59, 203n18

220n20. *See also* Partial-Peace
Plan; refugees, Palestinian
Palestinian state: Area C (West
Bank), **xv,** 155–156, 159,
222n2; East Jerusalem as
capital, 158, 223n6; Israeli
support for, 46–47, 198n16;
Palestinian rejectionism, 47,
102–103, 198n16, 209n10;
right of return (*haqq al-ʿawda*),
76–79, 148, 205n8, 206n11;
security concerns, 144–146,
152, 216nn7,8, 220n20; sovereignty of, 148–150, 209n8,
218n13, 219n14, 223n5
Palmach, 135, 137
Partial-Peace Plan, 215n4; Arab
state interests in, 152,
219n19; Divergence Plan,
141, 156–159, 163–164, 168,
222nn2,3, 224n12, 225n2;
impact on security, 146–147,
152–153, 220n20; in Islamic
law, 149–150, 219n16
PCPSR (Palestinian Center for
Policy and Survey Research),
180nn7,8
Peace and Security Association,
223n6
peace initiatives: Arab rejection
of, 43, 47, 100–103, 196n8,
198n16, 209n10; Camp David
Accords, 47–48, 103, 146–147,
192n26, 198n16, 219n17;
Clinton Parameters, 47, 103,

149, 210n11, 216n7; Disengagement Plan, 33, 57–60,
118–119, 202n14; Divergence
Plan, 141, 156–159, 163–164,
168, 222nn2,3, 224n12,
225n2; history of, 40–41,
43–45, 101, 196nn6,8,9;
impact of intifadas on, 32,
47–48, 199n18; Israeli public
opinion on, 13–14, 44–47,
119–120, 158, 196n9; Oslo
Accords, **xv,** 45–46, 108,
199n18; Palestinian refugees'
right of return (*haqq al-ʿawda*),
76–79, 205n8, 206nn11,12;
religious aspects of, 148–150,
218n13, 219n14, 219n16;
socialism, 30, 37–39, 40–46,
133, 135–136, 196n6, 198n13.
See also demographics; Partial-
Peace Plan
Peel Commission, 101
Peres, Shimon, 38, 45–46
PLO. *See* Palestinian Liberation
Organization
political Zionism, 116, 171, 182n1,
189n20, 190n21
Porat, Hanan, 56, 57, 202n12
pragmatism, 174–175, 214n4
princes (third generation of Israeli
right), 31–34, 35
psychological aspects of Israeli-
Palestinian conflict, 7–12,
31–32, 38, 74–79, 148,
204nn2,3, 218n12

Palestinian population in, 83, 143; Palestinian state including, 103; in Partial-Peace Plan, 220n20; settlement blocs, 217n11; withdrawal and impact on Jewish national identity, 111–112

San Remo Conference, 29

Sapir, Pinchas, 193n30

Saudi Arabia, 152, 219n19

Schechtman, Joseph, 182n3

Schlesinger, Akiva Yosef, 12–13, 181n16

Second Intifada, 47–48, 103, 198n17, 199n18

secular Zionism: dialogue with ultra-Orthodox community, 134–135, 137; Disengagement Plan, 58; Abraham Isaac Kook on, 53, 59; Zvi Yehuda Kook on, 54–55; nationalism of, 53, 59, 135; in the Redemption, 55, 58–59, 203n18; Shinui (centrist secular party), 196n6. *See also* Ben-Gurion, David

security: Allon Plan, 143–144, 145–146, 214nn1,2,3, 215n4, 216n9; demographics and, 32–34, 68–73, 82–83, 86–87, 138, 193n30, 207n5, 220n20; Disengagement Plan, 33, 57–60, 118–119, 202n14; fear in Jewish history, 7–10, 24, 38, 98, 180n10, 183nn2,3, 184n4; in Jordan Valley,

143–145, 215nn4,5, 216n7, 217n11; technological solutions for, 159, 223nn7,8,9; withdrawal from territories, 60, 68–69, 70–72, 107–110, 117, 211n9, 215n4. *See also* Partial-Peace Plan

settlement movement, 97, 147, 159, 217n11; settlement evacuations, 56–57, 109, 202n12, 220n20, 224n10; on withdrawal from the Land of Israel, 56, 107–109, 202n12

settlements: democratic character of Israel, 87–88; evacuations of, 56–57, 109, 202n12, 220n20, 224n10; Israeli Supreme Court rulings on, 209n1; Oslo Accords, **xv,** 45–46, 108, 199n18; religious aspects of, 54, 56, 57, 105–109, 202n12

Shamir, Yitzhak, 210n7

Shapira, Haim-Moshe, 19, 20, 182n2

Sharon, Ariel, 33

Shas Party, 107

Shavit, Ari, 47–48

Shavit, Yaacov, 189n20

Sher, Gilead, 220n20, 223n9

Shiite Arabs, 152

Shinui (centrist secular party), 196n6

"Shir LaShalom" (song by Rothblit), 196n9